Lord, Teach Us to Live

Jennifer Chamberlain

Bladensburg, MD

Lord, Teach Us to Live

**Published by
Dove Christian Publishers
P.O. Box 611
Bladensburg, MD 20710-0611
www.dovechristianpublishers.com**

Copyright © 2020 by Jennifer Chamberlain

Cover Design by Gerardo Garcia

All rights reserved. No part of this publication may be used or reproduced without permission of the publisher, except for brief quotes for scholarly use, reviews or articles.

Scripture quotations, unless otherwise noted, are from the ESV® Bible (The Holy Bible, English Standard Version®), copyright © 2001 by Crossway, a publishing ministry of Good News Publishers. Used by permission. All rights reserved.

ISBN: 9781734303223

Printed in the United States of America

To my mother, Jean T. Bailey, whose love,
support, and years of teaching Sunday School
truly taught me how to live.

Contents

Lord, Teach Us to Live vii

Chapter One
Our Father 1

Chapter Two
Who Art in Heaven 18

Chapter Three
Holy is Thy Name 33

Chapter Four
Thy Kingdom Come 52

Chapter Five
Thy Will Be Done on Earth as it is in Heaven 67

Chapter Six
Give Us this Day our Daily Bread 100

Chapter Seven
And Forgive Us Our Trespasses/Debts 113

Chapter Eight
Lead Us Not into Temptation 129

Chapter Nine
But Deliver Us from Evil 143

Chapter Ten
For Thine is the Kingdom and the Power and Glory Forever 158

Chapter Eleven
Amen (So Be It) 172

Lord, Teach Us to Live

Christ's disciples said, "Lord, teach us to pray," and as He taught them the Lord's Prayer, He taught us how to live.

These writings are intended to encourage those of us who follow Christ and seek a closer relationship with Him. Our Lord's words as He taught His disciples to pray give great insight into how we can live in this evil world and yet be separate from it.

First, let us look at the Lord's Prayer in its entirety. While researching the prayer, I found this beautiful translation from the Biblical Hermeneutics Stack Exchange. It claims to be a literal translation. Whether it is or isn't I do not know. What I do know is that it draws me deeply into the prayer, and I hope it touches you as well.

> Father of ours who's in heaven,
> hallowed be thy name of yours,
> come thy kingdom of yours,
> arise thy will of yours,
> as in heaven, also on earth.
> This bread of ours that's for the coming day
> give us this day.
> And free us from these debts of ours
> as also we have freed those debtors of ours.

And do not lead us into trial,
but draw us to you, away from that which is grievous.

There are a variety of translations of the Lord's Prayer. Many of us memorized the King James Version of Matthew 6:9-13 when we were young. It goes like this:

> **Our Father, which art in heaven,**
> **Hallowed be thy Name.**
> **Thy Kingdom come.**
> **Thy will be done in earth, as it is in heaven.**
> **Give us this day our daily bread.**
> **And forgive us our trespasses,**
> **As we forgive them that trespass against us.**
> **And lead us not into temptation,**
> **But deliver us from evil.**
> **For thine is the Kingdom,**
> **The power, and the glory, Forever. Amen.**
> (Some versions use the words "forgive us our debts as we forgive our debtors")

According to Andrew Brown, the religious affairs correspondent for the UK-based Independent News, there are two other versions used by the Catholic Church.[1] One is the modernized version of 1662 which, at the end, says, "the power, and the glory, forever <u>and ever.</u> Amen."

The other from the 1980 American Standard Bible goes like this:

> **Our Father in heaven,**
> **Hallowed be your name,**
> **Your kingdom come,**

---

1 https://www.independent.co.uk/news/uk/home-news/lords-prayer-to-be-given-in-three-versions-1411325.html

**Your will be done on earth as in heaven.
Give us today our daily bread.
Forgive us our sins
as we forgive those who sin against us.
Lead us not into temptation but deliver us from evil,
For the kingdom, the power, and the glory are yours
Now and forever. Amen.**

The Lord's prayer is listed twice in the Bible, once in the gospel of Matthew and once in the gospel of Luke. They are similar but vary for reasons which we don't need to go into except to say just a little about Luke and Matthew.

It is accepted that Luke (a doctor) was a Gentile and wrote His narrative of Christ's life and teaching 60 to 69 years after Christ's death and resurrection. He investigated and researched Christ's life and the creation of the church and wrote accordingly.

Matthew was one of the twelve disciples of our Lord. Matthew was writing his personal recollection of the life and words of Christ.

Here is Luke's version:

> "And it came to pass, that, as he was praying in a
> certain place, when he ceased, one of His disciples
> said unto him Lord teach us to pray, as John also
> taught his disciples. And He said unto them, 'When
> ye pray, say,
>
> *'Our Father, which art in heaven,*
> *hallowed be your name.*
> *Thy kingdom come, thy will be done*
> *as in heaven, so on earth.*
> *Give us day by day our daily bread,*
> *and forgive us our sins,*

for we also forgive every one that is indebted to us.
And lead us not into temptation
but deliver us from evil.'"
(Luke 11:1-4 KJV)

It is not important that the versions vary slightly or that there are many translations. They teach us to begin with praise, to ask for God's will, to ask for forgiveness, and to ask for His help to forgive others. We are taught to continue by asking for God's protection and deliverance and to end our prayer with praise again. This is a very unselfish prayer unlike those that we often hear today.

The value that we find in the Lord's Prayer is not just that it shows us a better way to speak to the God of creation, but that it shows us a better way to live our lives as Christ's followers. It speaks of God as our Father. It shows us a picture of Heaven and Holiness. It encourages us to look forward to His Kingdom and, while we wait, to do His will. It shows us about *needs* versus *wants* in our prayers and in our lives and reminds us to forgive as we have been forgiven by Him. It speaks of the evil that we face daily and how much we need His protection and guidance. And it reminds us how great is our God.

My prayer is that *Lord, Teach Us to Live* will encourage and strengthen the reader as I break down the parts of the prayer and write about the difficulties we face in our daily lives. May we always allow God to teach us through His word.

Jennifer

Chapter One

Our Father

The Truth about Fathers

But now, O LORD, you are our Father; we are the clay, and you are our potter; we are all the work of your hand (Isaiah 64:8).

God our Father is the perfect example of what an earthly father should be. He loves us unconditionally. He does not hold a grudge or remind us of what we have done in the past. He gives us what we need but not always what we want. He knows what is best for us but allows us to make our own choices. He comforts us when bad things happen, teaches us, guides us, and directs our paths if we listen to Him.

Some earthly fathers are good examples of God, loving and kind and willing to do anything for their children. Some never raise a hand in anger. They teach their children the difference between right and wrong.

Some fathers are the opposite and do not represent God. All over the world, there are fathers who are not in their children's lives at all due to divorce or abandonment. The type of father we have or had can color the view we have of our Heavenly Father. It is important for us to know who our Heavenly Father truly is and how much He loves us.

A father in the biological sense does not necessarily mean a father who cares for us. A biological father may not have any of the above listed good traits and often a non-biological father will. Depending on which type of father we have—one who is loving or one who is not—when we begin to form a relationship with God and His son Jesus, our earthly father's attributes may come to mind and cause us to think that He is like the father we have known in our lives.

If we have a loving earthly father, it is easier to see God as loving. If not, we struggle with the term 'God the Father,' remembering only the anger and cruelty of our own. We may think of God as one who punishes, a God of all *no's* who wants to spoil our fun or wants to beat us into submission. If we did not have a father growing up, we may not know what a father is supposed to be like and have difficulty developing a strong personal relationship with God.

If we have a negative view of fathers, we must put that away and know that God is loving and kind and wants only to give good gifts to His children.

The original Greek in the Bible pater – father;* means one who *imparts* life and is *committed* to it; a progenitor, bringing into being to pass on *the potential for likeness.

This definition says more than we might see at first reading. A father is one who **imparts life** whether biologically, spiritually, or emotionally. An adoptive, foster, stepfather, or grandfather can impart life in our hearts. Feeling loved and cared for by a father or mother figure can bring life to those who feel dead inside.

A good father is **committed** to the life of the one he loves and can cause that child to **become like** him. An evil father can do the same. We can become like either of them or we can become like our Father God, the one who truly **imparted life.** We can choose.

God created us and is committed to guiding us into becoming **more like Him**. When we were lost, He sent His son to redeem us and bring us back to Him. If we don't have a loving father here on earth, we always have a loving Father with us. He is **committed** to bringing about the best in our lives when we accept Him as our Father.

Every good gift and every perfect gift is from above, coming down from the Father of lights with whom there is no variation or shadow due to change (James 1:17).

Though God created all of us, many are separated from Him. There is one way to call God Father and that is by accepting the sacrifice of His Son Jesus and asking for His forgiveness of our bad choices, evil actions, and crimes—all of which are called sin. Turning away from them permanently and turning to God is how we allow God to truly be our Father.

"For God so loved the world, that he gave his only Son, that whoever believes in him should not perish but have eternal life" (John 3:16).

Believing in His Son Jesus is the way to eternal life with the Father. We read John 3:16 but focus our attention mostly on the last part. Believing is what brings us life eternal with God but what about the first part of the verse? Our Father loved the WORLD so much. He continues to love His creation, the world. The verse doesn't say that He loved US so much or CHRISTIANS so much. It says He loved the WORLD. He is the Father of the whole world which He created (**imparted life to**) and is **committed** to. He wants the whole world to become like Him as we were created in His image. He is the perfect Father.

One God and Father of all, who is over all and through all and in all (Ephesians 4:6).

A Father's Love Has No Bounds

Jesus Christ, God's Son, is also God just as the Holy Spirit is God. This is called the trinity. God is the Father. God is the Son, and God is the Holy Spirit. They are three in one just as we are body, soul, and spirit. We are created in His image in this way.

Do you not believe that I am in the Father and the Father is in me? The words that I say to you I do not speak on my own authority, but the Father who dwells in me does his works (John 14:10).

When we create something good like a work of art, it has value to us. We might even say we love it. The artist or creator wants to protect it because we know it intimately with all its strengths and weaknesses. We know what the best use of it would be and how best to handle it. We know how to pack it for mailing or as a gift. We want people to love it as much as we do.

God our Father created us. He knows everything about us. He knows our strengths and weaknesses and how we should be handled. He knows who we need in our lives and He knows what will make us stronger so that we can deal with this life. He created us and we are living creatures with the God-given capacity to love. He wants us to love Him just as He loves us.

The LORD your God is in your midst, a mighty one who will save; he will rejoice over you with gladness; he will quiet you by his love; he will exult over you with loud singing (Zephaniah 3:17).

God our Father never leaves us, and He never stops loving us no matter what we do. Even if we turn our backs on Him, He is there waiting for us to come back. When life causes us to stumble or we are hurting, He is there to pick up our pieces and put them together again. He is constantly trying to bring us into a close relationship with Him. We only need to call out to our Father.

For I am sure that neither death nor life, nor angels nor rulers, nor things present nor things to come, nor powers, nor height nor depth, nor anything else in all creation, will be able to separate us from the love of God in Christ Jesus our Lord (Romans 8:38-39).

It is not our Father who has caused the discord and evil in this world. The powers of darkness that currently rule over the earth try to draw God's creations away from Him and are working in every possible way to turn us from our true path. They lie to us about God, but still, He allows us to choose our own path because He has given us free will.

God has always wanted sinful man to have a loving beautiful relationship with Him as it was in the beginning. To bring us back into that relationship, He made the ultimate sacrifice by sending His son to die in our place. All we need to do is accept that He is our God and Father and that His son died in our place. All we need do is to ask for His forgiveness and His love will enfold us. He is waiting as a loving Father does for us to draw closer.

But God shows his love for us in that while we were still sinners, Christ died for us (Romans 5:8).

We don't have to be anything the world deems as special.

We are special to God because He made us. To return to Him, we don't have to be good enough or better in any way than we are right now. We only need to accept His gift and His love which is limitless and unconditional.

We show our gratitude and love back to God by the way we live in our songs, in our hearts, in our actions, and in our speech.

He is Always Here

Have I not commanded you? Be strong and courageous. Do not be frightened, and do not be dismayed, for the LORD your God is with you wherever you go" (Joshua 1:9).

God is always with us. Every person on earth, under the earth, in the sky, on the moon, or wherever they happen to be at any given moment, has God with them. This concept is challenging to grasp even for those who know the majesty and the omnipotence of God. For unbelievers it is impossible.

We may find it hard to believe that God the Creator of the universe would want to spend every minute standing by our sides, living in our hearts and loving us as though we never did anything wrong. We struggle to understand this love even knowing that the blood that was shed by Christ has cleansed us from our sins and redeemed us in His eyes. Believe!

The grace of the Lord Jesus Christ and the love of God and the fellowship of the Holy Spirit be with you all (2 Corinthians 13:14).

We are encouraged by the knowledge of His presence. We can be comforted to know we are not alone. It is difficult to understand how those who don't know God as Father get through their daily lives without being emotionally destroyed by the evil around them. Knowing He is here to help direct us and keep us out of troublesome situations lets us breathe in His peace.

Though many of us know He is here, we often don't behave as such. If Christ were physically with us, our actions would most certainly be different. Our speech would be kind and thoughtful and our pace unhurried so that we could stop and be helpful to those in need. Our diet might even change along with our sleep patterns, our rising, and our retiring for the night. The movies and the television shows we watch along with the music we listen to and the conversations we have with others might change drastically. We need to always be the person God wants us to be because He IS here with us.

Teaching them to observe all that I have commanded you. And behold, I am with you always, to the end of the age" (Matthew 28:20).

God wants His consistent guardianship and friendship to be a comfort, not a punishment and not a judgment. He loves us so much that He greatly desires our company. He wants to commune with us and have a relationship with us that is more than just one day a week. He instructs us, guides us, and gives us spiritual gifts and talents to use for His glory. He rejoices when we walk and talk with Him. He desires unceasing prayer. That means we can talk to Him constantly throughout our day.

If we view His attentiveness and persistence as negative, we need to rethink our values. What a comfort it is to know that God stands beside us when things are bad, not just when things are good. He is also seeking and speaking to those who don't know Him yet. He never gives up on anyone no matter where they are, what they have done, or what they are doing.

His Holy Spirit is with us. We have access to the King of Kings and all that He has to offer just for the asking. He is standing right here right now. We are strong with His might. We are fearless with His courage.

Today, we cannot count on anything in this world and this world gives us nothing, yet we seek everything it appears to offer. All we can truly count on is God our Father to be with us until the end of the age. Let us seek Him and acknowledge His loving care each minute, knowing that He is always here.

Fear not, for I am with you; be not dismayed, for I am your God; I will strengthen you, I will help you, I will uphold you with my righteous right hand (Isaiah 41:10).

Hearing the Father

When the Spirit of truth comes, he will guide you into all the truth, for he will not speak on his own authority, but whatever he hears he will speak, and he will declare to you the things that are to come (John 16:13).

God speaks to us, but do we hear? His ways of communicating are varied and many. Hearing Him can be a challenge and takes practice. To hear God, we normally would have a close personal relationship with Him. We must be in conversation regularly with Him and avoid doing all the talking (or asking). We must patiently wait for God to speak. We must listen with our spiritual ears and hearts.

If we are only approaching our Father with our needs and wants and if we are never still or listening for His voice, we will miss it. Though our Father could speak to us through very clear and miraculous ways, that is generally not how we hear from Him.

God speaks to us through His Holy Spirit to our intellect

(our mind), whom some call our soul (as in body, soul, and spirit). Whatever we call it, the more communication time we have with Him, the more we will learn to recognize His voice. Since He is always with us, we should always be ready to hear what He has to say.

The Holy Spirit also speaks to our spirit. We might call it intuition, conscience, or a gut feeling. We may feel led by the Spirit of God and this is another way that we 'hear' Him. If any of these 'feelings' are contrary to God's word, then we are not hearing Him but another voice. We can practice and learn to discern God's voice.

Beloved, do not believe every spirit, but test the spirits to see whether they are from God (1 John 4:1a).

"At the deepest level our spirit gives us meaning and purpose and our spirit enables us to love one another, our self and God. It's through our spirit that we have communion and fellowship with God. Our spirit gives us intuition between right and wrong" (Faith and Health Connection).

My sheep hear my voice, and I know them, and they follow me (John 10:27).

There are no tricks to hearing from God. He is our Father. He hears us when we talk to Him and He speaks plainly to us. However, when God does not talk back immediately or what we hear is not what we wanted, we may become frustrated and disregard it as not coming from Him.

We all hear from God, though we may not be aware that He is speaking. Sometimes He speaks through our conscience or through a song or through a message at church. Sometimes He speaks through others to confirm what we think we have already heard but are unsure.

Sometimes He speaks to us when we can't sleep, recalling

people who need prayer or revealing a message that He would like us to take to them. He doesn't only speak to us when we pray but when we listen.

And your ears shall hear a word behind you, saying, "This is the way, walk in it," when you turn to the right or when you turn to the left (Isaiah 30:21).

Reading our Father's messages in the Bible and communicating with Him about every aspect of our lives will determine how easily we recognize His voice over others. God's voice will never contradict His word. That is key. Other's voices will be worldly, unkind, contradictory, angry, or manipulative.

God is not sneaky. God is love. When the voice we hear is not filled with love, it is not God. In reading or listening to God's word, we will know the mind of our Father. When He speaks, we will know it is Him if it aligns with His word.

We often talk about asking God for wisdom and knowledge and yet have no idea how to recognize when those are given to us. We can be confident that God is giving us what He promised, but it is our responsibility to be able to discern His voice above the rest.

So faith comes from hearing, and hearing through the word of Christ (Romans 10:17).

Let us consider Romans 10:17, which is a verse some struggle with. Our faith is made stronger and our relationship with the Father becomes greater when we **hear** from Him. Faith comes from hearing. We hear from Him because we **read His word** and follow it (hearing through the word of Christ). The more we read, the more we hear and the greater our faith becomes. This life cycle brings both knowledge and wisdom, helps us recognize the voice of God, and fills us with His peace.

The accuser of this world the devil will try to speak but God will overpower that voice. Listen only to the goodness of the Father, the Creator of us all. His voice is only good. When good thoughts come, repeatedly pray about them and God will confirm them in your heart.

If He speaks a word for us to give to someone else that is encouraging and uplifting, we cannot be afraid to pass it on. An encouraging word will not do harm if we do not share it in pride as if we were special. If we go around telling people we heard from God, we are probably not hearing from God.

Hearing from God should make us humble. Our focus is on a stronger relationship with Him. We will hear from God in His time, not ours. As we become more mature spiritually, we will hear Him more clearly.

The fruit of His Holy Spirit, which are love, joy, peace, patience, kindness, goodness, faithfulness, gentleness, and self-control, will all come to us as we read His word, seek these fruit, and listen for His voice.

He Hears Us

And this is the confidence that we have toward him, that if we ask anything according to his will he hears us. And if we know that he hears us in whatever we ask, we know that we have the requests that we have asked of him (1 John 5:14-15).

It is important for us to hear God, but it is also very important to know that He hears us. Asking for things from our Father is not difficult, but careful thought should be put into how we pray and for what. Nevertheless, our Father hears us when we pray no matter what words we use, even if our request is not in His will.

We are used to asking for things. We are greedy and selfish

in our old human nature. We go to the Father and we know He hears us, but still, some of our prayers are answered with 'no,' 'not yet,' or 'not this way,' and that does not make us happy. Sometimes we begin to think He doesn't hear us at all.

Prayer is a big topic in the Bible. We are told how and when to pray, where and why to pray, and what to pray for. There are so many scriptures that *appear* to give us the magic key to answered prayer. We just need to do it right, right? Here are some parts of scripture that are often mistaken as a surefire way to get what we want. These are all parts of scripture taken out of context (This is sarcasm).

> ***Prayers of the righteous will be answered; pray for forgiveness; pray for daily needs; ask and it will be given you; believe and you will receive; call and I will answer; pray with thanksgiving; pray for each other; pray without ceasing; pray in secret; ask according to His will; don't use many and big words; pray for your enemies and those who hate you; pray for the government and the leaders; pray humbly; ask in my name and it will be given to you; pray with lifted Holy hands; pray that we won't be tempted; pray with faith and you will receive; and if two or more agree you will have what you ask.***

So, (facetiously) this is easy; we just need to be righteous, humble, forgiven, thankful, constantly in prayer in secret with small words but with at least two people with our hands up praying for each other, government, and our enemies with faith in accordance with His will and be sure to say "in Jesus name" before the Amen. Then we will have everything we want. No problem.

God hears prayers of all types and from everyone, not just those that follow what we sometimes perceive as the prescribed format. He loves for us to bring our needs to Him in any way we can. He wants us to fellowship with Him as any father would. God is listening to our hearts. The scriptures about prayer are to encourage us **to** pray, not to give us a magic formula for getting our prayers answered. For example:

Do not be anxious about anything, but in everything by prayer and supplication with thanksgiving let your requests be made known to God (Philippians 4:6).

God doesn't want us to be **anxious,** so we are encouraged to bring our needs to Him in prayer. Sometimes it seems that prayer is seen as money for a vending machine of blessings. But prayer is communication with our Father, our God, and our Lord. We should be in constant contact with Him throughout the day telling Him the good and the bad and asking for His will and guidance along the way. We should spend as much time in prayer as we do on our cell phones. *Ohhhh, that hurts.*

Our prayers become cries of desperation when we are in pain, worried, broke, or sick, and that is okay with God. He understands that we want the pain to end, the worry to be solved, finances to be provided, and health to be restored. He even understands when we are angry at Him. God is listening, and He cares.

The problem with prayer is ours, not His. When prayers are not answered in the way that we want, we feel let down by God. We may even be upset with ourselves for not having enough faith to bring the answer about in the way we prayed for it. We followed the formula, but we didn't get what we wanted. Didn't we have even a mustard seed of faith in us? Faith is strong and God does bless faith, but He also wants us to have what we need and those around us to have what they need. In sports, both teams don't win even when all the mothers on both sides have faith.

Therefore, I tell you, <u>whatever</u> you ask in prayer, believe that you have received it, and it will be yours (Mark 11:24).

In this scripture, it's all about the word "whatever." Word usage in the Bible needs to be understood in the context of the language of the day and how the people would have understood it. When writing their letters, the apostles knew their audience and what they would understand the word "whatever" to mean.

The word "whatever," when referred to in prayer to the newly formed churches of Christ, meant "whatever we ask for in accordance with God's will." The same goes for believing and faith. It doesn't matter how much we believe if what we are asking for is not in accordance with God's word and His will. The answer will be "no" if it is not in our best interest or in God's great plan for our lives.

Today, we use words in the same way. Meanings of some words are implied because we are familiar with the speaker or the subject. If our spouse is drinking a soda, and we ask, "May I have a drink?" He or she will not go get us water because they understand that we are asking for a drink of their soda. If they are eating and we ask for a "bite," they will not offer their arm for us to bite into; they will offer us a bite of their food. We do not have to be specific because we know they will understand what we are saying.

It is not necessarily our lack of faith or a lack of humbleness that makes or breaks our answer from the Father. God is not turning away because we prayed in the wrong way. His love for us is unending and unconditional. We are free to come before Him with every concern and desire. **John Piper** says it beautifully:

"We do not purchase answers to prayer by anything we say or do; we only plead for the overflow of mercy

already purchased by the sacrifice of our Lord."[2]

Pray without ceasing, (1 Thessalonians 5:17)

Father, I Want It Now

We live in a fast-paced world where immediacy is key to our existence. A seeming lack of faith is a byproduct of the speed at which we expect things to happen. We struggle with patiently waiting for our Father in Heaven to work out our situation or answer our prayer. We have become so used to instant gratification; we feel that God is very slow-moving. Scripture says He will deliver us, not that He will deliver us immediately. God is not a fairy godmother with a magic wand.

God is not slow nor is He fast. He is perfect. He is a loving Father who is working in the lives of every child He created. His desire is for all His children to return to fellowship with Him. If He were to work out our situation quickly, what would that do to the problems, prayers, and concerns of the person next to us?

The Lord is not slow to fulfill his promise as some count slowness, but is patient toward you, not wishing that any should perish, but that all should reach repentance (2 Peter 3:9).

If we have human fathers that love us and are good to us, we trust them. We might not always agree with them, but we trust that they have our best interest at heart. How much more should we trust and have faith in our Heavenly Father? Impatience does not necessarily show a lack of faith but is a

---

[2] John Piper, "What Do Answers to Prayer Depend on? Part 2. God's Will." https://www.desiringgod.org/messages/what-do-answers-to-prayer-depend-on-part-2.

negative attribute for which we should seek His help. He will give us more patience and faith without judgment.

He understands the world we live in. He understands the pain we feel during difficult times, and He knows that we wish they would be over sooner. Christ suffered all that we suffer and more and left His Holy Spirit to comfort us during these times. Rely on Him and watch for His next move.

Let us look at our pasts and see what God has done in times when we were impatient for Him to work. We need to remember the times we called out to God, "Why are you so slow?" and look at what He did in that situation. If we make ourselves aware of the times God worked out our situation, it will build our trust and faith in Him for the next time.

God doesn't promise that He will strengthen us right this minute or that He will help us in our desired way. He promises to strengthen us when we need strength and to deal with us in the way that is best, just as loving human fathers do.

God's truth is truth whether we like it or not. God's way is perfect even if it seems slow in coming. We can have hope, which is the assurance that God is working for our good. We might still expect immediate results from the world but, from Christ's teaching, we know that not all good things come to us quickly.

Rejoice in hope, be patient in tribulation, be constant in prayer (Romans 12:12).

When we are in the middle of waiting for an answer from God or for Him to act on our behalf, we can focus our minds and actions on doing good for those around us. In that way, not only will we be an instrument used of God in someone else's life, we will also turn our thoughts and concerns from focusing on ourselves. We can have confidence that God is constantly moving and acting on our behalf even if we don't see the results immediately.

> *And let us not grow weary of doing good, for in due season we will reap, if we do not give up (Galatians 6:9).*

We can rest in faith accepting that our Father loves us more than we know, and His ways and His will are better than ours. Lack of faith, anxiety, fear, impatience, and worry do nothing for our emotional or physical well-being. They do nothing to help our situation. They bring only pain and suffering.

Let us work for God in the lives of those around us, showing His great love. Let us breathe and smile, laugh and pray, even if our hearts are breaking, knowing that God only gives good gifts to His children. He will provide what we need when we need it.

> *For I know the plans I have for you, declares the Lord, plans for welfare and not for evil, to give you a future and a hope (Jeremiah 29:11).*

Chapter Two

Who Art in Heaven

Where is Heaven?

He will wipe away every tear from their eyes, and death shall be no more, neither shall there be mourning, nor crying, nor pain anymore, for the former things have passed away" (Revelation 21:4).

If we look up studies and discussions about heaven, we can become confused. Where is it? What is it? How and when do we go there?

All we really need to know is how. The other questions don't matter. Jesus said that if we believe in Him, we will not perish, and we will have eternal life with Him. That is all we need to know.

"For God so loved the world, that he gave his only Son, that whoever believes in him should not perish but have eternal life (John 3:16).

It might be interesting to study those other questions but if we are not careful, they can draw us away from what is truly important. Believing in Christ's death and resurrection are the keys to heaven, wherever it is. Scripture is meant to encourage and teach us, not frustrate and confuse.

Some people find deep research to be fascinating, and if they are grounded in their faith in God, there should be no problem. The difficulty is that these studies do not help us with our daily struggles and may not help us grow closer in our relationship with the Father. Christianity is simple and the gift of eternal life is free. Believe in Christ and His death and resurrection. Ask for His forgiveness and spend eternity with Him.

It is always helpful to know when reading scripture who is talking to whom, why, and what is happening at the time. However, in His wisdom, God created scripture such that, even taken out of context, it is able to encourage and strengthen us. Our amazing God knew we would need it both ways. To know about heaven, though, all we need to know is that we will be with God for eternity and it will be glorious.

But as it is, they desire a better country, that is, a heavenly one. Therefore, God is not ashamed to be called their God, for he has prepared for them a city (Hebrews 11:16).

There are many theories and beliefs among religions that place heaven in another dimension. Some say it is a holding place until the new earth and new heaven are created. Some say it is Eden. How it exists or where it exists is a discussion that could last for eternity. We won't truly know until we get there; so let's concentrate on getting there.

Again, these ideas, though perhaps interesting, do not matter. We can't allow vain discussions to draw us away from looking forward to our place with Christ. We desire not only God's love and mercy here but an afterlife with no pain or suffering because that is what was promised and what we have when we accept Christ's death on the cross for our sins.

In my Father's house are many rooms. If it were not so, would I have told you that I go to prepare a place for you? (John 14:2)

Here is what we know for certain. Jesus promised us eternal life with Him. He promised that He was going to prepare a place for us. He said it is His Father's house, so He and His Father (God) will be there. There will be no more pain or sorrow. We will see God as He is. We will know Him as He is meant to be known. There will be no death or decay, and it will be beautiful.

And the twelve gates were twelve pearls, each of the gates made of a single pearl, and the street of the city was pure gold, transparent as glass. And I saw no temple in the city, for its temple is the Lord God the Almighty and the Lamb. And the city has no need of sun or moon to shine on it, for the glory of God gives it light, and its lamp is the Lamb. By its light will the nations walk, and the kings of the earth will bring their glory into it, and its gates will never be shut by day— and there will be no night there (Revelation 21:21-25).

Our God has prepared a place for us. We want to go there and live with Him forevermore. It is simple. Have faith that Jesus died for your sins, confess your sins before Him, and do your very best to live for Him each day. Heaven will be waiting, no matter where it is.

Who goes to Heaven?

Jesus said to him, "I am the way, and the truth, and the life. No one comes to the Father except through me"

(John 14:6).

It may seem clear that those who believe will enter heaven and live eternally with God. But even the fallen angels believe. Satan believes, and he will not be spending eternity with God. How can that be? What are we missing?

Different churches stress different instructions from the Bible. Some say baptism is the only way into heaven. Some stress doing good works as the only way into heaven. Some encourage organized religion and going to a specific church as a requirement to get into heaven. Who goes to heaven if just believing is not enough?

For by grace you have been saved through faith. And this is not your own doing; it is the gift of God, not a result of works, so that no one may boast (Ephesians 2:8-9).

Getting into heaven is not difficult but it does require one thing: faith. We can have the assurance that we are going to be with God forever no matter what we have done in our past. He sees our hearts. He sees what we believe and what we think and what we feel about Him. It is not ours to earn by baptism or good works or even church attendance. No one can live a sin-free life. The gift of salvation and entrance into heaven is a free gift to those who are justified by faith in Christ.

The word *belief*, when speaking of accepting Christ as our Lord and Savior, is part of faith in Him and in following Him. We can have belief without faith, but we cannot have faith without belief. Believing that something exists does not necessarily change the way we live our lives. But having faith in someone means we trust and rely on them. They are an integral part of our lives.

In the case of Christianity, our belief in Jesus and His death and resurrection and our belief that God created this plan to bring us back into fellowship with Him creates faith in our hearts. We know that we can depend on God to guide and direct our lives and to take us to live with Him for eternity. It is our hearts that show where our faith lies, and it is the faithful who go to Heaven.

The Bible, the word of God, makes it very clear **how** we can get to heaven. Jesus is the only way to God. When He took our place on the cross and died, He made a way for us to be forgiven of our sins. When Christ died and rose again, we became eligible to have our sins forgiven by believing (having faith) and becoming a follower of Him.

> *"Abraham believed God, and it was counted to him as righteousness." Now to the one who works, his wages are not counted as a gift but as his due. And to the one who does not work but believes in him who justifies the ungodly, his <u>faith</u> is counted as righteousness (Romans 4:2-5).*

Eternal life with Christ is a gift from God to be accepted with open hearts. We show our faith and commitment by doing as He commanded but if we miss something or mess up, we don't fear that we will be rejected by God. He will never turn away and He will show us what is right. Reading His word and prayer is the way to grow our faith to know God's heart and be assured that our eternity will be in heaven.

There are many verses in the Bible that tell us how we should live once we believe and have faith. We should forgive others the same way that we have been forgiven by God. We should love God and keep His commandments. We should love our neighbors. We should obey the Son. But these are not the keys that open heaven's doors. Faith in Christ and His forgiveness of our sins is how we get to see God. When we have faith and forgiveness, our hearts' desire is to serve. The service is a joyous outcome of being forgiven and accepted by

God but is not the way into Heaven.

For the wages of sin is death, but the free gift of God is eternal life in Christ Jesus our Lord (Romans 6:23).

Others may try to get us to follow man-made rules about what we should eat, wear, or do. These rules may be helpful for us, but they will not get us into heaven. God sees our hearts. If our hearts are right with God, we will go to heaven.

A Hard Truth

Jesus answered him, "Truly, truly, I say to you, unless one is born again he cannot see the kingdom of God" (John 3:3).

Not everyone gets into God's Kingdom, what we call heaven. This is a true and powerful statement and may make people uncomfortable and even question God's love. God is clear in His word about both His love and heaven. He clearly loves us, and He clearly made a way for us to enter heaven for eternity. He also gave us free will so that we could choose His way or follow a different path. Not making a choice to follow God <u>is a choice</u> to *not* follow God and will preclude those who make it from spending eternity with God.

We have a benevolent and fair Father in Heaven who loves us and is merciful, but He is also the King of all and there is only one way to spend eternity with Him. In His fairness, only those who come to Him through Christ will be welcomed into Heaven where His Kingdom is now. He has thrown out the life preserver. All we must do is take it. God does not reject humankind or send anyone to hell. Humankind rejects God's gift.

He will not welcome or give His promise of eternal life to those who continually sin without repentance. Those who do not accept His gift and follow Him will not be allowed to enter God's Kingdom even if they are *really* good and nice people. <u>This is a hard truth.</u>

> ***For by grace you have been saved through faith. And this is not your own doing; it is the gift of God, not a result of works, so that no one may boast (Ephesians 2:8-9).***

We Christians know God is our loving Father. He walks with us daily, helps us avoid temptation, forgives our sins when we ask Him, and guides our paths. We don't like to think of Him as a King who would allow our loved ones to spend eternity without Him in misery and despair. It might seem to contradict what we have been taught about His nature, but it does not.

We all understand the concept of suffering the consequences of our actions. God is perfect and perfectly fair. What He says, He will do. If He did not keep His word, following Him would be chaos and no one would have the certainty of salvation.

We must stop sugar-coating Heaven just because it is difficult for us to understand hell. Although God loves everyone and wants everyone to accept Him, love Him, and ask Him to forgive them of their sins, some will choose another path. This is their choice, not God's. Salvation through Christ is based on faith, not works, so even those who dedicate their lives to helping the poor will not go to heaven if they have not given their hearts to God.

God our King has given and continues to give all people every opportunity to believe in Him and to accept His son who died for us. Since God in His perfection cannot tolerate sin, He must see us through the blood of Jesus which makes us white as snow and perfect in God's eyes.

> ***"Not everyone who says to me, 'Lord, Lord,' will enter the kingdom of heaven, but the one who does the will***

of my Father who is in heaven" (Matthew 7:21).

God is so merciful that He has delayed His return so that everyone has an opportunity to hear the good news and follow Him. He will give eternal life to everyone who accepts this gift. He will accept the very young and those who pass away without the ability to make this choice for themselves. But to those who choose not to believe and those who make no choice at all, eternal life without God awaits and that is hell.

Because, if you confess with your mouth that Jesus is Lord and believe in your heart that God raised him from the dead, you will be saved (Romans 10:9).

God has given us one requirement to enter heaven and told us of the consequences of not meeting that requirement. Since it is a gift, many may think it doesn't involve a conscious choice. It does. We must choose to follow God and His teachings through Jesus Christ. Think of this again; no choice is a choice not to follow God's one requirement and there is no other God that we can follow that died for us and offers this gift.

Jesus said to him, "I am the way, and the truth, and the life. No one comes to the Father except through me" (John 14:6).

This is painful for us because we all know someone who passed from this life and may not have given their heart to God. Do not fret or be sad. Though each must decide to follow Christ we do not understand God's mercy and we cannot see into a person's heart as they are dying. We can pray that God was able to reach them at the end. All things are possible with God and we know that He does not want any to perish so we hold fast to hope for these people though some will not make it. How much better it would have been if they had lived their lives for the Lord.

We also have a responsibility as followers of the King to understand His requirements. We must reach out while we are here to make sure that others accept the truth of God and His son before the end of their time on earth. That is the only way to be certain we will see them again.

But the LORD is the true God; he is the living God and the everlasting King. At his wrath the earth quakes, and the nations cannot endure his indignation (Jeremiah 10:10).

We have gotten soft. Though we know the truth of salvation it is easier to believe that everyone we know will be in heaven. We need to tell the truth about salvation to the people we know and love. We must somehow make them understand and give their hearts and lives to God. We must stop tickling our ears with what we want to hear.

For thine is the kingdom, and the power, and the glory, forever. Amen (Matthew 6:13).

Heavenly Decisions

Multitudes, multitudes, in the valley of decision! For the day of the LORD is near in the valley of decision (Joel 3:14).

The decisions we make today determine where we will spend our eternity. Will we be with God or apart from Him in misery? In this life we make decisions. Some of them are unimportant and have no real impact on our lives but others are a matter of life and death. Such is the decision we make about God. It is the most important decision we must make.

Many people go through life thinking they have plenty of time to decide about God. Maybe He exists; maybe He doesn't. Heaven isn't real. Hell is here on earth. No big deal. I'll decide later. However, not making a conscious choice to believe in God and all that He has told us is a decision not to follow God. There is no half-way. The undecided life leads to destruction and eternity without God.

I call heaven and earth to witness against you today, that I have set before you life and death, blessing and curse. Therefore choose life, that you and your offspring may live (Deuteronomy 30:19).

Think of this lifetime as lasting one day and eternity as lasting 100,000 years. In this one day, we must decide where we will spend the 100,000 years. We only have one day to decide and then we will spend the next 100,000 years in one of two places. We only must make one choice because if we don't choose God then we default to the other place. We call eternity with God Heaven and the only way to choose to go there is to accept Christ and the salvation He provides.

We can choose to believe in God, follow Him during this one day, ask Him to forgive our sins and help us in this one day, or we can choose not to believe in God. We can also ignore the whole decision-making process, which then becomes the decision.

Choosing God means we will spend 100,000 years in peace where there will be no pain or suffering, no crying, and no evil. Spending the next 100,000 years with God requires a conscious choice to follow Him, but anything else, any other decision, or no decision means we will spend the next 100,000 years without God. Without God, there will be misery and suffering and more pain than we have ever known. We only have this lifetime (this day) to decide and we never know when this day will end.

> *But now, O LORD, you are our Father; we are the clay, and you are our potter; we are all the work of your hand (Isaiah 64:8).*

God created the universe and He created us. Everyone knows you can't get something from nothing, so we know the universe was created. If it was created, there must have been a creator. God is who we call the creator. The word *god* means a divine being or, from the Jewish word *Yahweh*, the one who is.

Once we have made the decision to believe in God the creator, we can then believe what He has told us in His word, the Bible. His words have been proven true by the recorded prophesies (predictions) that have come to pass over thousands of years.

A decision to believe in God means we believe that He sent His son—literally, His word—in human form to suffer the punishment and death for past, present, and future crimes against God.

> *And the Word became flesh and dwelt among us, and we have seen his glory, glory as of the only Son from the Father, full of grace and truth (John 1:14).*

Believing in God means believing that Christ rose from the dead, in part, to show us that we will also be resurrected after death to eternal life with Him. Our decision will determine whether we will live eternally with God in heaven or eternally apart from God in what we call hell.

He created us with the free will to make this decision because He wanted us to believe in Him and to follow Him freely. The first of His creation made a bad decision from the very beginning, and the world has continued to disregard His instructions ever since.

Each of us has a decision to make, and He will continue

to gently prod us, showing us His truth along the way and urging us to make the right decision until our last breath.

> *And if it is evil in your eyes to serve the* Lord, *choose this day whom you will serve, whether the gods your fathers served in the region beyond the River, or the gods of the Amorites in whose land you dwell. But as for me and my house, we will serve the* Lord *(Joshua 24:15).*

This life is our opportunity to choose where we will spend eternity. It doesn't matter what church we attend or what day we worship. It doesn't matter how we dress or the songs we sing. The only thing that matters is our decision. Have we decided to believe and asked our Father to forgive us for those wrongs He died for?

When we make the decision to believe and follow Him, He will come into our hearts (as His Holy Spirit), and we will have a relationship with Him as our Father.

> *For with the heart one believes and is justified, and with the mouth one confesses and is saved (Romans 10:10).*

If we decide by faith to believe and follow our Creator and His son Jesus Christ, we will have made the right decision and will be assured of eternal life with God that is a lot longer than 100,000 years. We will be righteous in God's sight.

> *And these will go away into eternal punishment, but the righteous into eternal life (Matthew 25:46).*

Get Serious about Heaven

> *He will wipe away every tear from their eyes, and death shall be no more, neither shall there be mourning,*

nor crying, nor pain anymore, for the former things have passed away (Revelation 21:4).

When we first accepted Christ into our hearts and lives and decided to follow Him, we were very excited and may have told everyone how wonderful it was to be a Christian. We didn't want anyone to miss out on eternity in Heaven with God. The time that this excitement lasted was different for everyone, but over time it faded away; for some, slightly; for others, a lot.

We need to get that excitement back. Eternity in Heaven is still in the balance for many of our family and friends.

For those who have accepted Christ, Heaven is waiting, but our Father wants more from us than holding our own salvation to ourselves. It is not enough to just be Christians, pray, and attend church. We are called to spread the good news of the gospel.

Many Christians go no farther, having decided that just by living a decent life, other people will know how great God is and that everyone will go to heaven. That is not true, and we know it. People may see we are different, but this lie we tell ourselves because we are scared or lazy and our passion has faded will not bring anyone into the Kingdom of heaven.

Do not lay up for yourselves treasures on earth, where moth and rust destroy and where thieves break in and steal, but lay up for yourselves treasures in heaven, where neither moth nor rust destroys and where thieves do not break in and steal. For where your treasure is, there your heart will be also (Matthew 6:19-21).

We may think that laying up treasure in heaven is the prayers we've prayed or the committees we've chaired for the church. However, treasure in heaven is what we have done for our Father who is there. He desires that we bring others into fellowship with Him so that they can spend eternity in heaven too.

As Christians, we are to be dedicated to the service of God. We are holy people set apart for His use. We serve our Father who lives in Heaven.

Over time, our initial excitement of knowing that God loves us tends to wane. We still go through the motions of what being a Christian means to us. We believe in God. We talk to Him, sometimes. We put on a good show at church, pray, sing, and participate in church activities. The rest of our time is spent in worldly pursuits and worries.

He has told us to read His word, gather with other believers, pray unceasingly, do good, and tell the world about Jesus. This is how He wants us to be separate from non-believers and bring others with us to heaven. These things take time and effort, but we are selfish, and we are afraid. Our Christianity becomes a once and done thing.

Why? Because we want to fit in. We don't want to be considered strange or religious fanatics. We don't want to be ridiculed, laughed at, pushed out of the group, or not accepted. We might even lose our jobs.

We need to look around at the world and see the sin that is now considered acceptable. We need to see the hatred, anger, and misery of people who don't know the truth. Do we want all of God's children to have a relationship with Him before the end comes, or not? We will never do anything for God if we settle for complacency in our own relationship with Him.

The revelation of Jesus Christ, which God gave him to show to his servants the things that must soon take place. He made it known by sending his angel to his servant John (Revelation 1:1).

It is time to get serious about heaven. Christ will return and, in the meantime, everyone around us will eventually die. The time is now. He is the way. He is the truth. He is in Heaven and that is where we want to be along with all our loved ones. He saved our lives from death and eternal life in hell. Our complacency may allow someone to die in sin.

We need to take our beliefs seriously. It is time to tell others about Heaven.

> *But as it is, they desire a better country, that is, a heavenly one. Therefore God is not ashamed to be called their God, for he has prepared for them a city (Hebrews 11:16).*

Chapter Three

Holy is Thy Name

Only God Is Holy

Therefore, if anyone cleanses himself from what is dishonorable, he will be a vessel for honorable use, set apart as holy, useful to the master of the house, ready for every good work (2 Timothy 2:21).

Holiness is one word for sanctification. The word *sanctification* is used by some churches and not by others, mostly because it can be a confusing subject and lead to vain discussions that draw us away from actually being holy. We know that only God is truly Holy or perfect, but His word directs us to try to obtain holiness as much as it is humanly possible.

> *Sanctification: Hagiazó: to make holy, consecrate, sanctify. Original Word: αγιάζω. Phonetic Spelling: (hag-ee-ad'-zo) Short Definition: I make holy, sanctify. Definition: I make holy, treat as holy, set apart as holy, sanctify, hallow, purify (Strong's Greek Concordance).*

Notice the varied meanings in the original Greek for *sanctification*. The use of this word in scripture can imply these different meanings. *Making holy, treating as holy, purify,* and *setting apart as holy* are very different things. We can surmise that this is the reason sanctification is often the source of disagreements among various Christian groups.

In the long run, it probably doesn't make any difference what we believe about the word sanctification if we, by the Holy Spirit, are constantly trying to live a life that is Christ-like.

We would need to study the specific meanings in the various verses to be able to determine the best interpretation for that scripture. This may be of interest to some, but for most of us, it may be better to cleanse ourselves from all that is dishonorable and to focus on the new life that Christ has given us. In short, God is Holy; try to be like Him.

Some believe that sanctification is a progressive work or that we are a work in progress once we accept the Lord and believe in Him. Some believe that we can achieve complete sanctification while on earth or be sanctified from the moment we become a Christian. Then there are those who believe we can achieve complete sanctification during times of crisis (like Stephen when he was stoned), but afterward, continue to be imperfect as before and our sanctification becomes progressive again.

> *And such were some of you. But you were washed, you were sanctified, you were justified in the name of the Lord Jesus Christ and by the Spirit of our God (1 Corinthians 6:11).*

This world is difficult enough without struggling with definitions of words like sanctification.

We can decide for ourselves if the use of the word is something we need to be concerned about. We believe and follow Christ, and we are continually striving to be like Him. When we see Him, we will be like Him (or fully sanctified). Often, too much time concentrating on these issues distracts and draws us away from focusing on Christ and how He would like us to live.

> *Now may the God of peace himself sanctify you completely and may your whole spirit and soul and body be kept blameless at the coming of our Lord Jesus Christ (1 Thessalonians 5:23).*

When we decide to believe in God and the gift of His sacrificed son for our sins, we ask for forgiveness. Our sins are then forgiven, but we are still not perfect. We follow Christ; we are set aside for God's use, ready for every good work, which is, indeed, a definition of sanctification. Unfortunately, as humans living in a sinful world, we fail.

Is sanctification like trying to find the perfect church that, as soon as we join, is not perfect anymore? What can we simple Christians say about the subject of sanctification? Most of us are not Bible scholars. What we know is that God is Holy. We have accepted that Christ died in our place for our sins and we are forgiven and set aside for good works in His name. This is what we need to know.

We need to praise and worship our Holy God and do the best we can to follow His example. Ask for forgiveness when we fail, then get up and try again. We are set apart for His use so we need to allow ourselves to be used by Him. Only God is truly Holy.

What Sets Us Apart as Holy

> *We are afflicted in every way, but not crushed; perplexed, but not driven to despair; persecuted, but not forsaken; struck down, but not destroyed (2*

Corinthians 4:8-9).

We face challenges in life. We have worries and trials. Family matters, jobs, friends, finances, and church responsibilities take up our time and energy. In these ways, we are just the same as non-believers. The differences between Christians and others are what we believe and how we respond to these challenges in life.

Do not be anxious about anything, but in everything by prayer and supplication with thanksgiving let your requests be made known to God (Philippians 4:6).

We should not be anxious, because we know that our Holy God is meeting our needs. We may not always be successful in having complete faith, but by our prayers and through our relationship with God, we communicate with Him and develop the assurance that He loves us and is active in our lives.

God does not leave us alone to work out our challenges without Him. We have a God and a Creator who loves us and wants what is best for us as we love and follow Him. We are different from the world, and they will not understand, but this is what sets us apart and shows them a different way to live.

> *Count it all joy, my brothers, when you meet trials of various kinds, for you know that the testing of your faith produces steadfastness. And let steadfastness have its full effect, that you may be perfect and complete, lacking in nothing (James 1:2-4).*

Within the loving arms of Jesus, we have joy in our trials and challenges and believe that He will make our faith strong so that we can stand firm when difficult times come. We believe that the world should know how great our God is and how confident we are in His care.

We meet the same trials as others in this world. We suffer loss, we ride the emotional roller-coaster of relationships, we have sicknesses, we lose our jobs, and we are afraid. Though we experience all of this and other emotions, we don't let them overtake us. Being set apart means that our future is safe, and each time we move through a trial, we will grow stronger in our relationship with the Holy Father.

We do not believe everything is random, that we evolved from monkeys or anything else, or that there are many paths to salvation. We believe the word of God, and we follow His teaching. We feel His strength when times get tough. We bear one another's burdens and pray for each other. We draw strength from the body of Christ. We are different, and if we are not different, there is a serious problem.

I can do all things through him who strengthens me (Philippians 4:13).

We can do what God wants us to do, and we strive to do it. Through His strength, we will get through even the worst of trials. He will never let us down. This sets us apart as Holy.

There is therefore now no condemnation for those who are in Christ Jesus (Romans 8:1).

Our sins are forgiven. Christ died in our place and rose from the dead. When we die, we will spend eternity with Him, and our lives should show this certainty to those who have not accepted Him into their hearts and lives. This sets us apart as Holy.

We all have challenges in life, but it is how we react to them that makes us different and set apart as Holy. We have a helper in the Holy Spirit because our God is Holy. We have a Father who gives us good gifts and protects us. We have a

Brother who saves us. We have the love of our brothers and sisters in the body of Christ. We have eternal life with God.

We are set apart to be Holy as God is Holy.

Worthy of Praise

Through him then let us continually offer up a sacrifice of praise to God, that is, the fruit of lips that acknowledge his name (Hebrews 13:15).

Praise is important to our Holy God. He is worthy of our praise just because of who He, not because of what He does for us. We are blessed daily in our walk with Christ, but Christianity is not all about what we get out of it.

Praising God is about Him and His blessings apart from what He does for us. It is not about our needs or wants. It is all about God and who He is. We praise Him because He is the Creator, the Lord of all, the Lamb of God, and the Light of the World. There is so much to praise Him for that has nothing to do with what He can do for us.

Thanksgiving is also pleasing to God, and we should readily thank Him for His blessings. But many of us are lacking in our praise and thanksgiving. Fortunately, God does not sit on His throne and complain about how little we respect and admire Him, but He does desire our gratitude, not because He needs it, but because it is spiritually healthy for us.

Let them praise your great and awesome name! Holy is he! (Psalm 99:3)

Webster's Definition of Holy is:

exalted or worthy of complete devotion as one perfect in goodness and righteousness.

God's very name and the name of Jesus are Holy and worthy

of our praise. He is perfect, and He is righteous. He deserves our continual praise and worship because He is Holy.

We need to include praise and worship into our daily prayers. The Lord's Prayer begins with praise: "Our Father, who are in heaven, **Holy is your name**." Beginning our prayers with praise and glory to God frees us from focusing on our own selfish desires. Each time we realize and acknowledge how great God is we become less centered on our own needs and more grateful for the salvation, protection, and guidance He gives us.

> *Praise the* L*ord*! *For it is good to sing praises to our God; for it is pleasant, and a song of praise is fitting. The* L*ord* *builds up Jerusalem; he gathers the outcasts of Israel. He heals the brokenhearted and binds up their wounds. He determines the number of the stars; he gives to all of them their names. Great is our Lord, and abundant in power; his understanding is beyond measure (Psalm 147: 1-5).*

Praise and worship are easy at church when we are singing and clapping. Someone else is leading us in praise and prayer, and we just follow along. At home in our private prayer time, we may find it more difficult to glorify God, as all we can think about are our problems and concerns. We may not know what to say. We may not feel like praising Him. We have things to ask for and we want to get right to it but beginning with praise opens doors in our hearts that we don't even know are closed.

Taking time to praise and worship God on our own, though it may be awkward at first, brings peace and relief during struggles and joy and confidence that all will be well. We can start with just a simple sentence of "God I praise you for who you are." The Holy Spirit will take it from there. We will feel the presence of God in a more tangible way when we praise Him.

> *Praise the L̲ord̲! Praise God in his sanctuary; praise him in his mighty heavens! Praise him for his mighty deeds; praise him according to his excellent greatness! Praise him with trumpet sound; praise him with lute and harp! Praise him with tambourine and dance; praise him with strings and pipe! Praise him with sounding cymbals; praise him with loud clashing cymbals! (Psalm 150:1-5)*

God enjoys our praise, and His word says He inhabits our praise. That is why we feel closer to Him when we offer up praise and worship. He is always with us, but when we exalt Him and show our complete devotion, He is pleased. We draw closer in our personal relationship with Him and that is always the goal.

Even as human beings (though this is a very shallow comparison), when we feel that someone deserves to be exalted, trusted, and loved, our relationship with them is stronger. When people only ask us for favors, our relationship is based only on needs and wants and doesn't usually last too long.

God is always with us and will never leave us. He answers our prayers but sometimes not in the way we would like. If we only spend time with Him asking for favors and feel that He is not doing what we ask, we may draw away because we don't have a true relationship. If we begin our prayers by praise and worship, we will realize His majesty and we will be humbled by His great love and grace. We are more likely to realize that our wants are not needs and that He has been working all things for our good. We can trust Him because He is Holy.

> *Praise the L̲ord̲! Oh give thanks to the L̲ord̲, for he is good, for his steadfast love endures forever! (Psalm 106:1)*

A Holy Name

The Lord's Prayer says, 'Our father, who art in heaven, hallowed (holy)' be thy name'. God's name is Holy. There is power in the name of our God and His son Jesus Christ.

Pray then like this: "Our Father in heaven, hallowed be your name (Matthew 6:9).

Historically a person's name is very important. Our names and reputations are either bad or good. Having positive characteristics associated with our name lets others know whether they can trust our word.

Because God's name is good and Holy, we know we can trust His word the Bible. We can trust Him. He is faithful and just and has a good and Holy name.

Names are made up of letters. They are how we identify each other. Names are given to us by others and some have meanings that may impart characteristics to us, the holder of the name. Names can be made fun of or ridiculed and become an embarrassment. Names can be recognized by all and be respected and adored. Certain names carry with them certain accomplishments or riches, and good names can be easily lost by human actions and words. But how can a name be Holy?

A good name is to be chosen rather than great riches, and favor is better than silver or gold" (Proverbs 22:1).

God is omnipotent. He is everywhere and in everything. He is His word. He is His name. His name is not just letters, and He is called by many names. He is the great I Am; Jehovah; Messiah; Prince of Peace; King of Kings; God of Abraham, Isaac, and Jacob; Yahweh, and many more. Each name is Holy because it represents the only one who is truly Holy.

This mystery is incomprehensible to us that God _is_ all and is _in_ all. The great mystery is that the many names of God not only represent Him but <u>are</u> Him. His name is Holy and powerful just as He and His word are Holy and powerful. We can call out His name and His power is there. He is there.

In the beginning was the Word, and the Word was with God, and the Word <u>was</u> God (John 1:1).

We have been given this great gift, the name of God's Son, who is one with the Father. We carry the prestige of the name of Christ because we are designated as Christians. This name represents our Holy and powerful God, and we should be honored to be called by this name.

It is our responsibility to show the world that this name is good. When we sin or represent the name of God in a bad way, we have dishonored our Lord and King. This is a heavy responsibility in a world where evil reigns and the name of God is blasphemed regularly.

So will I ever sing praises to your name, as I perform my vows day after day (Psalm 61:8).

Christians are to honor God's name, bring glory to His name, pray in His name, and live our lives so that others will also esteem His name and believe that His word is true. We can show confidence and faith in God's promises because of His powerful name. God will never lose His good name, but we can cause others to lose faith in Him by what we do in His name. The world is watching and finding fault with everything that Christians do and say. Do not give the enemy an opportunity to slander the Father.

And whatever you do, in word or deed, do everything in the name of the Lord Jesus, giving thanks to God the Father through him (Colossians 3:17).

If His name is Holy, our actions our lives and our words

should also be Holy. Living a true Christian life shows the Holiness of God's name. If we do not live a true Christian life, we are taking His name in vain by our lifestyle. Protect the name of God and His son Jesus Christ by keeping His good name Holy.

> *God said to Moses, "I AM WHO I AM." And he said, "Say this to the people of Israel, 'I AM has sent me to you'" (Exodus 3:14).*

Representatives of Christ's Holy Name in Prayer

> *Truly, truly, I say to you, whoever believes in me will also do the works that I do; and greater works than these will he do, because I am going to the Father. Whatever you ask in my name, this I will do, that the Father may be glorified in the Son. If you ask me anything in my name, I will do it (John 14:12 – 14).*

Christ and the Father are one. Therefore, Jesus is also Holy, and His name is Holy.

Following the last supper, Jesus said these words from John 14 to the disciples. He was reassuring them that even though He would be gone, they would be able to continue His work as His representatives and do even greater miracles than He had performed, so that God would be glorified.

The disciples were extremely worried about His leaving, and they really didn't understand what was going to happen. Jesus was calming their fears and letting them know that whatever they did as representatives of Him (in His name), His power would be behind it. They would have, in His name, great power to do His work.

Today the phrase 'in Jesus' name' at times has lost its meaning. It is used at the end of every prayer no matter what the prayer is about. Though God probably is not offended, it may serve us to give it some thought.

Perhaps we have never understood what Jesus truly meant when He told His disciples that whatever they asked in His name, He would do. Remember that He was speaking to the disciples at a crucial junction of His ministry.

> *Christ here assures them that they should be clothed with powers sufficient to bear them out. As Christ has all power, they, in his name, should have great power, both in heaven and in earth. I. Great power on earth (v. 12): He that believeth on me (as I know you do), the works that I do shall he do also. Though he should depart, the work should not cease, nor fall to the ground, but should be carried on as vigorously and successfully as ever; and it is still in the doing.*[3]

Ending every prayer with the phrase 'in Jesus' name' seems to have become some sort of magic saying that will make our prayers come true.

Jesus was very clear to His disciples that when they were out doing His work and performing the miracles that He performed as long as they were doing the works as His representatives in His name, He would accomplish it so that the Father would be glorified in the Son.

When we pray for help going to sleep at night or for help at our jobs, these are not the works that Christ was speaking about though I'm sure asking 'in Jesus name' will not hurt the cause.

When Christ taught us to pray what we now call 'the Lord's Prayer,' He did not say 'in Jesus' name' at the end of it.

---

[3] Henry, Matthew, "Exposition of the Old and New Testament, Volume 3," Tower & Hogan. London, 1828.

Christ's words to His disciples are surely also meant for us, and the reasoning behind His words remains the same. We must be doing the works that Christ would do if He were here, and we must do them as His representatives because He is not physically on earth. We are His hands and feet.

When we pray for healing or salvation, we are doing the work of the Lord and He will be glorified. We can pray in the power of the name of Jesus to accomplish these works. We also need faith and we also need to be praying for the will of God.

> *You did not choose me, but I chose you and appointed you that you should go and bear fruit and that your fruit should abide, so that whatever you ask the Father in my name, he may give it to you (John 15:16).*

When we are bearing fruit for the Father we are doing so as representatives of Jesus Christ His Son. We are not doing good works for our own glory or to gain salvation through them. We have been appointed just like the disciples to go out into the world and preach the Good News just as Jesus did. We do these things in His name.

> *In that day you will ask nothing of me. Truly, truly, I say to you, whatever you ask of the Father in my name, he will give it to you (John 16:23).*

Jesus provides for us His power and His wisdom to do the works that He is no longer physically here to do. But our prayers do not always need to and should not end with 'in Jesus name' without consideration or serious thought. Those words need to have meaning.

Only those prayers that are truly for the glory of God through His Son's death and resurrection and that are not for our wants or for selfish gain should be prayed in the name of Jesus. Prayers of praise and adoration, prayers of minor consequence for ourselves, or prayers to open and close meetings need not have that phrase before the Amen (so be it).

We know that God gives grace for our human frailties and probably does not mind if 'in the name of Jesus' is used constantly. But our prayers are communication with God and they are important. The name of Jesus is so powerful that we ought to give it some thought and not just rattle it off at the end of every prayer.

No Evil in Our Holy God

For you are not a God who delights in wickedness; <u>evil may not dwell with you</u> (Psalm 5:4).

We often hear that God cannot look upon sin. We may have said it ourselves. We use that phrase because it simplifies things for us. It makes it easier to explain why God's son was sent to cleanse us with His sacrificed blood. God cannot accept us when we are sinful.

But this phrase makes God seem weak and we know that He is not. God is all-powerful and can do anything, see anything, and be anywhere. He can look at sin and at sinners and does so daily when He looks at the world. What we mean when we use that phrase is that God is perfect and Holy and there is no evil in Him. Evil cannot dwell with Him; therefore, we cannot live eternally with God if we have not been forgiven for our sins by accepting the sacrifice of His Son on the cross.

Any evil close to God would be burnt up by His glory and perfect goodness. We would be more correct if we said that sin or evil cannot look upon or be near God. We, unless our sins are forgiven, will not be allowed in God's presence.

After our monumentally bad choice in the garden of Eden

and the destruction of our relationship with God, something had to be done to repair the damage. God wanted the same closeness with us that He had with Adam and Eve, but the world was evil and had turned away from God. So, He made a way for us to be cleansed.

The law that God gave to Moses required blood sacrifice for sin. God sent Jesus in bodily form to shed His blood as the final blood sacrifice for the sins of the world, thus creating a way for us to dwell with God. Since that time, no additional blood is required to be shed. Christ's sacrifice for us only needs to be accepted as we ask His forgiveness for our sins.

For our sake he made him to be sin who knew no sin, so that in him we might become the righteousness of God (2 Corinthians 5:21).

Jesus' blood cleanses us from our sin so that we can have a relationship with our perfect God with whom evil cannot dwell. Jesus was and is God and He not only looked on sin, He lived with sinners and took our sin upon Himself on the cross. By accepting that truth, we can dwell with Him here and for eternity.

If we confess our sins, he is faithful and just to forgive us our sins and to cleanse us from all unrighteousness (1 John 1:9).

Sin separates people from God. Until a person has asked Jesus to forgive their sins, they are evil and not worthy to dwell with our Holy and perfect God. Jesus' death and resurrection make those who accept Him worthy. It is not something we can earn no matter how 'good' we, or the world, think we are.

When we believe and ask Jesus to come into our lives and forgive our sins, His blood that was shed on the cross covers us. Though blood is red, Christ's blood washes us and

God sees us as the purest white. We are worthy to be called children of God and all that we do should be for Him.

Yet for us there is one God, the Father, from whom are all things and for whom we exist, and one Lord, Jesus Christ, through whom are all things and through whom we exist (1 Corinthians 8:6).

All things are *from* God and all things exist *for* God. All things exist *through* Christ including us. We are to live our lives *for* Him allowing the love of Christ to flow *through* us to the world. We must make the choice to be forgiven and to live abundantly *through* Jesus Christ.

Where Has Holiness Gone?

Do not be deceived: "Bad company ruins good morals" (1 Corinthians 15:33).

Morality, as some of us have known it, is gone. Holiness seems far away. But God remains Holy and wants us to be Holy as He is Holy.

Many have been convinced by politics, television, books, movies, and songs that some 'wrongs' are really 'not that bad.' Watch a bit of news these days and see the anger, hatred, and distrust among our leaders, families, and friends. See them convince humankind that what God calls sin is not sin at all.

We are all human beings created by the same God, and yet, our morality has been split into a million pieces. Even churches split, and one becomes conservative while one becomes liberal. Revival must come now by the inviting of the Holy Spirit, God's Holiness, into our churches.

The biggest influences in the losing of morality are the statements that appear logical if we don't look too deep. Those who say women should have control of their own bodies seem to make sense until we realize that women's bodies are not theirs alone when they are carrying a child.

We should be able to love who we love, right? But that means men with men and women with women, which we know is an abomination to the Lord.

Schools say children need self-esteem, and they do, but some have taken it too far and created a totally self-focused generation who believe that whatever they want and enjoy is their right. No more do we think of others before ourselves or love our neighbors as we love ourselves. Where has Holiness gone?

> ***Do nothing from selfish ambition or conceit, but in humility count others more significant than yourselves. Let each of you look not only to his own interests, but also to the interests of others (Philippians 2:3,4).***

In today's world, those who speak the loudest and longest are the ones who are listened to. Technology allows all to be heard all the time. They make the news; they cause protests in the streets that become violent, and eventually, the world falls in line with their thinking.

The result of listening to those who speak the loudest without checking what they say against the word of God is that the world is drawn more deeply into sin. The result of believing that whatever feels good is good is sin. The world has gradually embraced sin as acceptable. It is being taught that long-held beliefs based on the Bible are not applicable today. But God does not change.

> ***Now the works of the flesh are evident: sexual immorality, impurity, sensuality, idolatry, sorcery, enmity, strife, jealousy, fits of anger, rivalries, dissensions, divisions, envy, drunkenness, orgies, and***

> *things like these. I warn you, as I warned you before, that those who do such things will not inherit the kingdom of God (Galatians 5:19-21).*

Sex means nothing. Dressing provocatively and speaking vulgar language makes one popular. Yelling and fighting, drama and chaos swirl around in family units, between neighbors, and in our government. Drugs and alcohol, swapping spouses, 'identifying as the opposite sex,' lying to avoid discomfort, and taking what we want even if it doesn't belong to us is the norm today.

God has warned us, and if we as Christians do not take this warning seriously and continue to strive to be Holy as He is Holy, we will not inherit the Kingdom of God. If we do not take the evil that has pervaded this world seriously, we will not survive the persecution that is already upon us. God is not mocked.

> *God is not man, that he should lie, or a son of man, that he should change his mind. Has he said, and will he not do it? Or has he spoken, and will he not fulfill it? (Numbers 23:19)*

The Bible is the Holy word of God. It is truth. It does not change with the times. Even though there are a variety of interpretations, sin remains sin in all of them. God is God in all of them. The world may have lost its way, but we must remain steadfast following the truth and living our lives accordingly no matter what the world may say about it.

Evil, hatred, immorality, and all sin have no place with us or in the church. If we believe that what we are doing is wrong in the eyes of God (judging only our own behavior) for us it is sin. Stop doing it. It may not be easy, and it may not be popular with our group of friends, but we must live for God alone, have faith in God alone, and believe in God alone.

The world has lost its moral compass. We must make sure

that ours is true to course, or we will drown in the sea of filth that is all around us. The flood of Noah's time is nothing compared to what is happening to kill the world and destroy souls now.

> *Owe no one anything, except to love each other, for the one who loves another has fulfilled the law. For the commandments, "You shall not commit adultery, You shall not murder, You shall not steal, You shall not covet," and any other commandment, are summed up in this word: "You shall love your neighbor as yourself." Love does no wrong to a neighbor; therefore love is the fulfilling of the law (Romans 13:8-10).*

We can fulfill the law of God by loving not only those who agree with us but those who don't. Only by showing God's love in difficult situations can we see change come about. Arguing and fighting do not produce change. We must be the change. We must be holy. We must stay the course even when those around us think we are fools to do so.

God is Holy and all-powerful, never changing, and has complete and unconditional love for everyone. We must fight the powers of darkness that are overtaking the world. We must ask the Holy Spirit for more of every gift and fruit that God will provide to maintain our walk with Him among those who are enemies of God, some of whom are in our own families.

> *Do your best to present yourself to God as one approved, a worker who has no need to be ashamed, rightly handling the word of truth (2 Timothy 2:15).*

Chapter Four

Thy Kingdom Come

Thy Kingdom Come

There are a lot of verses in scripture referencing God's Kingdom. The most common of all is in the Lord's Prayer where we were taught to pray "thy kingdom come."

Why did Christ add this to the prayer and instruct us to pray for God's Kingdom? When will it happen and what does it mean? From Strong's Concordance, we have a translation from the original Greek.

> *basileia: kingdom, sovereignty, royal power, dominion*
> *Original Word: βασιλεία, ας, ἡ*
> *Part of Speech: Noun, Feminine*
> *Transliteration: basileia*
> *Phonetic Spelling: (bas-il-i'-ah)*
> *Definition: kingdom, sovereignty, royal power*
> *Usage: kingship, sovereignty, authority, rule, <u>especially of God, both in the world, and in the hearts of men</u>; hence: kingdom, in the concrete sense.*

When we accept the truth of Christ and His salvation, God's

Kingdom, His authority and rule, enter our hearts. When we die, we enter the Kingdom in Heaven. When He returns, Christ will reign over His Kingdom here on earth. When we pray the Lord's Prayer, we are asking for His Kingdom to come soon to the world, for His Kingdom to rule our hearts daily, and for us to enter the Kingdom when we leave this world. His Kingdom is both now and in the future. It is in Heaven and in Christians on earth and it will be on the new earth when Christ returns.

We are not experiencing God's Kingdom in the 'world' yet. When Christ died, rose again and ascended into heaven, He said He would return. We pray for that Kingdom especially. Come, Lord Jesus.

> *Jesus answered, "My kingdom is not of this world. If my kingdom were of this world, my servants would have been fighting, that I might not be delivered over to the Jews. But my kingdom is not from the world" (John 18:36).*

There was a lot of confusion in Christ's time because the prophecies seemed to speak of Him as a reigning King. Many expected that He would overthrow the government and usher in His Kingdom right then. They didn't understand that His death on the cross was for our sins and was the final blood sacrifice under the law of Moses. His sacrifice had to be accomplished to bridge the gap between us and God.

He told His disciples what would happen, but they just couldn't wrap their heads around it, having been taught the scriptures about His Kingdom all their lives. But we know the truth. We have a Kingdom to look forward to and we have His Kingdom ruling our hearts and minds when we accept Christ and follow Him.

> *Being asked by the Pharisees when the kingdom of God would come, he answered them, "The kingdom of*

God is not coming with signs to be observed, nor will they say, 'Look, here it is!' or 'There!' for behold, the kingdom of God is in the midst of you" (Luke 17:20-21).

When Christ said the Kingdom of God is in the midst of you, he was talking about Himself. He was the Kingdom and He was with them, but He had to die and return to heaven so that we could be saved and have the Kingdom through His Holy Spirit in our hearts.

What this means for us is that we must show the Kingdom of God to the world through our lives, and we must continue to pray that Christ's Kingdom will come soon to the world in the last days.

But that is not all. For Christians, the Kingdom of God is ours when we leave this earth and we ascend to the Kingdom of Heaven. We can look forward to being in His Kingdom when we die. It is our desire to enter the Kingdom of the Lord and to do that, we must believe that Jesus is the Son of God and live our lives for Him not only in lip service but in trueness of heart. We are all sinners, but as believers in Christ, we are forgiven of our sins and cleansed by the blood of Jesus, not by what we do, but by our relationship with Him.

Not everyone who says to me, 'Lord, Lord,' will enter the kingdom of heaven, but the one who does the will of my Father who is in heaven (Matthew 7:21).

When we pray the Lord's Prayer, saying, "Thy Kingdom come," we are asking for His Kingdom in our hearts and His Kingdom to come soon. We are rededicating ourselves to Him and affirming that we are ready to enter His Kingdom in Heaven. The world does not understand. They are no longer looking for a king as in the days of Christ nor do they have hope in the Kingdom of Heaven. They are blind and will die in their sins unless we tell them about the Kingdom.

And he answered them, "To you it has been given to know the secrets of the kingdom of heaven, but to them it has not been given" (Matthew 13:11).

There is so much that is difficult for us to understand and much that we will find we have gotten wrong, but we need to continue to seek always the Kingdom that will be when Christ returns, the Kingdom that exists now in Heaven, and the ability to show the Kingdom in our hearts when we are born again.

Jesus answered him, "Truly, truly, I say to you, unless one is born again he cannot see the kingdom of God" (John 3:3).

We need to remember that Jesus came to fulfill the prophecies about His Kingdom and that the final Kingdom is not here yet. We can enter it when we die if we live for Him and believe. One day, He will rule over all creation. He will come again as He promised. His Kingdom will come. We need to be ready. We need to be watchful. We need to live as Christ lived and show the world His Kingdom within us so that they, too, may enter the Kingdom and have eternal life with Christ.

And the LORD will be king over all the earth. On that day the LORD will be one and his name one (Zechariah 14:9).

Eagerly Waiting for the Kingdom

And while they were gazing into heaven as he went, behold, two men stood by them in white robes, and said, "Men of Galilee, why do you stand looking into heaven? This Jesus, who was taken up from you into heaven, will come in the same way as you saw him go into heaven" (Acts 1:10-11).

Jesus Christ is coming again. His Kingdom is coming. He told us He would come, and He keeps His promises. We don't know when. It could be today or tomorrow or fifty years from now, but we know He is coming, and we are not ready. We are not looking up. We are looking down at ourselves and at the world. We need to look up expectantly and pray for His Kingdom to come.

The Bible predicts that some will try to determine the day and time, but it cannot be determined. We who believe God's word know that the time of His coming is not to be known by us but that we are to be prepared and eagerly waiting. It seems that we as a church body are no longer eagerly waiting.

So Christ, having been offered once to bear the sins of many, will appear a second time, not to deal with sin but to save those who are eagerly waiting for him (Hebrews 9:28).

Unfortunately, this subject is often avoided because of its unpredictability. When we don't know something, we tend not to talk about it. But this lack of discussion is part of what makes us unprepared. This lack of interest in His coming and our preoccupation with our own lives and problems keeps us from setting our hearts and minds on God. It also makes bringing others to Christ of less importance.

We might not understand it all, but we can concentrate on what we do know. We know that He will come again because He said He would. We know that he will come in the same manner that He was taken up into heaven. We know that He will come when He is not expected and when the world is falling apart.

> *But the day of the Lord will come like a thief, and then the heavens will pass away with a roar, and the heavenly bodies will be burned up and dissolved, and the earth and the works that are done on it will be exposed (2 Peter 3:10).*

There have been many times when Christians felt that Christ's coming to earth was imminent and yet He did not come. The more this happens and the more we neglect to talk about His coming and look for it, the more unprepared we will be. But those people were right in one sense. Christ may not have come in the clouds, which He will in time, but none of us are guaranteed tomorrow so Christ is coming for each of us. We still need to be ready.

The powers of darkness that rule this world use God's patience in coming to sow doubt in the minds of believers. And this is just another excuse for unbelievers to convince themselves that there is no God.

The world is falling apart. Not only are there wars among countries but also among people within our own countries. Earthquakes, tornadoes, and strange weather occurrences are happening daily. Evil is prevalent. Strong Christian beliefs are wavering. True Christianity is diminishing. Many don't believe He is coming. Seemingly strong Christians are denouncing their faith and falling away.

This is so sad.

> *Therefore you also must be ready, for the Son of Man is coming at an hour you do not expect (Matthew 24:44).*

When we think of the second coming of Christ, we think of the Book of Revelation, which could easily be called the most confusing of all the scripture. But there are many other scriptures and words of Christ Himself that speak of His coming again. Christ's second coming is prophesied in Daniel,

Isaiah and in Jude.

> *It was also about these that Enoch, the seventh from Adam, prophesied, saying, "Behold, the Lord comes with ten thousands of his holy ones, to execute judgment on all and to convict all the ungodly of all their deeds of ungodliness that they have committed in such an ungodly way, and of all the harsh things that ungodly sinners have spoken against him" (Jude 1:14-15).*

We need to remember that Christ is coming again, and this time He is coming as a King, not as a shepherd. He is coming to take His children home and to reveal and destroy Satan. We ask for His Kingdom to come and it will come. We need to prepare ourselves, our hearts, our families, and our friends for this day.

We need to revive our spirits and stop centering our lives around this world. Our lives must center around Christ so that we not only show His love to those around us now but are ready when He comes to take us home. Complacency must be eliminated if we are to bring others into the Kingdom.

Will we stop avoiding this subject because it is confusing, or will we trust that Christ said He is coming and begin to look for Him? This is an exciting time. We should be singing and praising God because we know the end of evil is near.

> *He who testifies to these things says, "Surely I am coming soon." Amen. Come, Lord Jesus! (Revelation 22:20)*

Our Hope of the Kingdom

> *Having the eyes of your hearts enlightened, that you may know what is <u>the hope to which he has called you,</u> what are the riches of his glorious inheritance in the*

saints (Ephesians 1:18).

The word 'hope' is thrown about in conversation but has a much different meaning than in Biblical times. Today we might say "I hope you get that job", or "Hope you have a good day." We have no idea if these things will happen, but there is always 'hope.'

At times, we hold hope inside ourselves looking forward to better times and brighter days. 'Hope' used in this way is optimistic but also uncertain. We have a great desire but don't know if it will come to pass.

Life would be depressing without this type of 'hope,' but it is not the 'hope' talked about in Scripture. In fact, in God's word, 'hope' is just the opposite. It is a certain knowledge or a belief and expectation that God's promises will be kept. 'Hope' in the Bible means trust and confidence. Strong's Concordance lists hope this way:

elpis: expectation, hope
Original Word: ἐλπίς, ίδος, ἡ
Part of Speech: Noun, Feminine
Transliteration: elpis
Phonetic Spelling: (el-pece')
Definition: expectation, hope
Usage: hope, <u>**expectation, trust, confidence**</u>.

Paul, a servant of God and an apostle of Jesus Christ, for the sake of the faith of God's elect and their knowledge of the truth, which accords with godliness, <u>in hope of eternal life, which God, who never lies, promised before the ages began</u> (Titus 1:1-2).

A Christian's hope is what the Kingdom of Jesus Christ is all about. Christ is our hope of eternal life in His Kingdom. Throughout the Scriptures, humanity's hope was in the redemption promised by God and brought to completion through Christ. They believed with certainty that God would accomplish what He promised, and He did.

The Old Testament speaks about people having hope in God. Their hope was in salvation through a Savior that was promised to come. The people who were living under the law of Moses believed in the coming of the Savior. Prophesies told of the Christ and the salvation He would bring. They believed the promises of God. They were not 'hoping' the Christ would come as we would 'hope' today. They were waiting in expectation with confidence.

Today our hope is in Jesus, our hope of glory. God's plan to redeem us through Jesus, the Christ, has come to pass, and we have opportunity to accept or reject salvation through Him. Our hope—our certain knowledge—is in Him, in the salvation He offers us, and in eternal life in heaven.

This hope gives us peace through the struggles in our daily lives. We know that our struggles will end. We know we will spend eternity in His Kingdom. We are waiting in anticipation, knowing that what is said in Philippians 1:21 is true for us. **To live is Christ, and to die is gain**.

> *Blessed be the God and Father of our Lord Jesus Christ! According to his great mercy, he has caused us to <u>be born again to a living hope through the resurrection of Jesus Christ from the dead</u> (1 Peter 1:3).*

Every generation of believers has had this type of hope, knowing that God was working to bring us back into a right relationship with Him. Before Christ, people's hope was in God for the coming Savior. Today, we know the Savior has come. We hope in Christ who came as promised and died for our sins. It is interesting to see the promises of God unfold from Genesis to Revelation.

It is this hope, this certain knowledge of salvation, that we need to understand and to share. We are not living our lives as Christians and following Christ's teaching because we 'hope' (today's hope) that what He taught might be true. We are not silly people basing our entire lives on a 'maybe.' We are confident in God's word. We know His Kingdom is in us and will be coming soon with Christ as King.

Those who fear you shall see me and rejoice, <u>because I have hoped in your word</u> (Psalms 119:74).

Understanding Biblical hope as we read God's word helps us have confidence in our beliefs. Knowing that the writers defined 'hope' not as wishing but as assurance, strengthens our faith. We cannot be worried or uncertain when our hope is in God.

To them, God chose to make known how great among the Gentiles are the riches of the glory of this mystery, <u>which is Christ in you, the hope of glory</u> (Colossians 1:27).

Compassion, Showing the Kingdom

Blessed be the God and Father of our Lord Jesus Christ, the Father of mercies and God of all comfort, who comforts us in all our affliction, so that we may be able to comfort those who are in any affliction, with the comfort with which we ourselves are comforted by God (2 Corinthians 1:3-4).

Compassion is sometimes difficult to feel and even more difficult to show. Showing compassion is vitally important in today's world as we deal with hard-hearted people blinded by evil. We must practice and show Christ's compassion to everyone. We cannot only ask for His Kingdom to come someday; we must ask for His Kingdom to be in us and flow through us to others who are hurting.

God's eyes shine on us with compassion when we are in

pain. We cry out to Him, and He comforts us in our affliction. He wraps his loving arms around us, and we can feel His presence. And from His compassion for us, we learn to be compassionate to others. Compassion is one way we can show the Kingdom.

God's comfort is like a deep breath of fresh air. It sustains us. We know that He feels and understands our pain and loves us. We read about His compassion in the Bible and we feel it in our daily lives. It is the most precious part of His love for us. This is the Kingdom of God for those who believe.

But we also need that sensitivity and tenderness from the people around us when we are heartsick. We need our loved ones to hold us and to treat us with love and concern. When we cry out, we need warmth and tolerance from those around us just as we need it from the Lord. We need His Kingdom to come to us through other believers from the body of Christ. We also need to be the ones to give it when it is needed by others.

When he went ashore he saw a great crowd, and he had compassion on them and healed their sick (Matthew 14:14).

When Christ saw His children lost and emotionally distraught, He had compassion on them and healed them. We can just imagine the love He felt and His arms reaching out to hold them. That is what we want, not only from Him, but from our brothers and sisters. And we want to be the ones to show compassion to others. Christ in us is the manifestation of His Kingdom.

If someone shows us compassion, they take part of our load onto themselves. But when there is no compassion or understanding, our burdens become heavier, and though we know Christ is with us, we still can feel alone.

Bear one another's burdens, and so fulfill the law of Christ (Galatians 6:2).

We are a part of God's Kingdom, so with God, we do not feel isolated and lonely. But to suffer a lack of compassion from other Christians who are also part of the Kingdom makes our hearts heavy with sadness. We leave wounded, afraid and grieving.

Being aware of this and having suffered this lack of compassion, we must not be the ones who leave others wounded and grieving. We want the Kingdom from others, so we must offer it to them also.

Finally, all of you, have unity of mind, sympathy, brotherly love, a tender heart, and a humble mind (1 Peter 3:8).

Christ has compassion on us all the time. We need to have compassion for each other whether we understand the pain being suffered or whether we understand how someone got involved in a situation. Whatever is causing the pain doesn't stop the love and compassion from Jesus, and it shouldn't stop love and compassion from us.

We must support each other, love each other, pray for each other, and lift everyone's hurts to the Lord, who heals. We must investigate our hearts and see if we are truly compassionate and would go out of our way to comfort someone, even when we don't understand their pain. Are we showing the Kingdom that resides within us?

Rejoice with those who rejoice, weep with those who weep (Romans 12:15).

Our Treasure Field

The kingdom of heaven is like treasure hidden in a field, which a man found and covered up. Then in his joy he goes and sells all that he has and buys that field (Matthew 13:44).

Most of us love finding treasure, something unexpected that makes us happy. Some people make a living out of seeking lost earthly treasure, and it is exciting when they find something. Even the search brings anticipation and pleasure.

If Christians were asked where we place our treasure or what our most valued part of life is and then to list them in order of importance, we would likely list God, family, job, hobby, pets or similar.

If then, we were asked to honestly list the five things on which we spend most of our time and effort in order from most to least, our list might look quite different. Perhaps our list would be job, family, hobby, pets, and church. Understandably we spend most of our time either on work, sleep, and on the things that bring us pleasure.

Our treasure is not what we think is important but on what we want and on what we spend the most time.

And he will be the stability of your times, abundance of salvation, wisdom, and knowledge; the fear of the LORD is Zion's treasure (Isaiah 33:6).

God has told us to labor and to support our families and that we deserve our wages. Though He will supply our needs, He still expects us to do our part. The things we spend time on with our family and friends are not wrong in His eyes either, but often our pleasure is the center of our treasure. What we take pleasure in, like going out to eat or sewing, even spending time with our grandchildren, can become our focus instead of God.

With so little time for all the things seemingly necessary in this world, our Godly treasure can be pushed aside or even lost altogether. Isaiah says that the fear of the Lord is Zion's treasure. Fear of the Lord means respect. Respecting the Lord and seeing Him as our true treasure means He will provide stability, salvation, wisdom, and knowledge. These are indeed treasures needed in today's society.

> *Your gold and silver have corroded, and their corrosion will be evidence against you and will eat your flesh like fire. You have laid up treasure in the last days (James 5:3).*

God knows that we live in a world that requires a considerable amount of time on things that are not about Him. **However**, He is with us always and we can and should acknowledge His presence in all we do. Every activity should be done while we talk and sing and laugh with God. Our families would then see where our true treasure lies.

If others see that our time is spent more on the Internet than in the Bible, more on texting than listening to their needs and concerns and praying, more on accumulating wealth than on giving it to the needy, they will know that our treasure is here on earth.

> *Do not lay up for yourselves treasures on earth, where moth and rust destroy and where thieves break in and steal, but lay up for yourselves treasures in heaven, where neither moth nor rust destroys and where thieves do not break in and steal. For where your treasure is, there your heart will be also (Matthew 6:19-21).*

When we seek to accomplish goals that He was not the center of and the effort fails, that may tell us that we were not where God wanted us to be. Our efforts for God will be much more successful, and only the treasure we have built up for the Kingdom of God matters.

Worldly rust and moths will destroy what we do and what we own here. Those things are unimportant.

Storing up treasure in heaven is not all about time spent but is also about what we will and will not give up, what we keep in our hearts, and where our thoughts constantly land. If we find that there is something in our lives that we cannot give up to God, it might have become a treasure that is not in the Kingdom of Heaven.

Keeping God in our hearts and minds during all other activities and being able to cease those activities if the Holy Spirit impresses us or the word of God tells us to will ensure that our treasure is what it should be and is being stored in the proper place.

Our treasure hunt is in heaven. The field of riches that we seek is heaven. We must rid ourselves of earthly activities that possess us and, instead, possess that field of heavenly treasure at all costs.

And here is a reminder for those who have been blessed with riches here on earth.

> *As for the rich in this present age, charge them not to be haughty, nor to set their hopes on the uncertainty of riches, but on God, who richly provides us with everything to enjoy. They are to do good, to be rich in good works, to be generous and ready to share, thus storing up treasure for themselves as a good foundation for the future, so that they may take hold of that which is truly life (1 Timothy 6:17-19).*

Chapter Five

Thy Will Be Done on Earth as it is in Heaven

Christ's Will for Unity of the Body

Eager to maintain the unity of the Spirit in the bond of peace (Ephesians 4:3).

Sometimes the unity of the Body of Christ is affected by the differences among us. Some may feel they don't have any gifts or callings, are envious of others, or even discouraged. Some may feel unduly proud because of their special gift or look down on those who aren't participating in church projects.

God gave gifts to His people so that we could help build up His church corporately and each other individually. His will is for us to love Him, spread the Good News, build up one another, bear each other's burdens, commune with Him, and love each other as we love ourselves.

Every member of the Body of Christ has received God's call and yet we maintain our individuality and our talents or gifts. He knocked at our door until we answered. His will was for us to accept His truth and the gift of His Son. Once we accepted God's call to salvation, we became part of the Body of Christ, but we did not all become the same. That is where unity becomes difficult.

Each of us has other callings from God as well. He has willed some to preach, teach, and/or pray. We all have strengths in various areas, and we are all unique.

> *And he gave the apostles, the prophets, the evangelists, the shepherds and teachers to equip the saints for the work of ministry for building up the body of Christ until we all attain to the unity of the faith and of the knowledge of the son of God, to mature manhood, to the measure of the stature of the fullness of Christ (Ephesians 4:11-13) ESV.*

Not every member of the Body is gifted to do the same thing, but God wants us to work together in unity for His Kingdom. God will allow us to do something outside of our calling if it needs doing and there is no one else that will answer the call, but the Body runs more smoothly if everyone does what they are good at and what God has called them to do.

It is when we try to do everything, even those things we are not called to do (or do nothing), that the bonds of unity are pulled apart. When some don't use the gifts given to them or when others can't stop themselves from being involved in every aspect of the body, jealousy and strife will ultimately raise up. Leadership in the Body often allow this to happen because they need help and only a few are willing. The burden then becomes too great on some, and others hide out and miss the blessings that come from using their gifts.

God doesn't switch our gifts back and forth. Our gifts remain the same even though we may use them in different ways or on different projects. Our gifts — whatever it is that God has given us the desire and ability to do — will always be there whether we do them or not. It may take time to discover what our abilities and callings are from God, but through growth in our relationship with Him, our gifts will become clear and we can help build the unity of the Body.

Do nothing from selfish ambition or conceit, but in humility count others more significant than yourselves (Philippians 2:3).

God's will for unity among the Body of Christ is so very important. If the Body of Christ is in disarray, we will not be able to accomplish what God has set before us. We will not be able to show the world a better way.

The Body is always called to be kind. We who know what our gifts are should kindly and gently assist those who are seeking to find theirs. We can encourage those who are ignoring their gifts to join us in projects until they become confident and know what God is asking of them.

So if there is any encouragement in Christ, any comfort from love, any participation in the Spirit, any affection and sympathy, complete my joy by being of the same mind, having the same love, being in full accord and of one mind (Philippians 2:1).

None of us is without fault. No one's gift is so great, not even the preacher's, that other gifts are not needed. Let God take each person through their own learning process to find what He wants of them. Be kind and bear one another's burdens. Restore those who are discouraged.

If you don't know what your gift is, start with prayer. People who pray are always needed in the Body of Christ, and God will bless us when we give our time in prayer.

Finally, brothers, rejoice. Aim for restoration, comfort one another, agree with one another, live in peace;

and the God of love and peace will be with you (2 Corinthians 13:11).

"Christian-speak": Furthering God's Will

As Christians, we forget that religion has its own language, and we throw it out there thinking that everyone will know what we are talking about. In order to further God's will for all to come to Him, we must be careful of our 'churchy' language, especially around those who were not raised in a church. We can bring about God's will on earth by changing our language to reflect the meaning of terms instead of throwing around words that mean nothing to many.

This language barrier is one of the devil's means of deception. How can we reach people if they don't know what we are talking about? Nice try Satan! God always reveals to us what we need to reach those He loves and wants to bring into a close relationship with Him.

'Sin,' 'Satan,' and 'devil,' among others, are words used by Christians among other believers because we know what those words mean, but we should try to avoid these words in non-believer settings because people will not only scoff at them but will not fully comprehend what we are trying to tell them.

What words can we use that are 'non-Christian speak' in place of these words that are less likely to be misunderstood and/or shut off the ears of those we are speaking to? Do we ourselves fully understand these words enough to use other phrases?

So whoever knows the right thing to do and fails to do it, for him it is <u>sin</u> (James 4:17).

The original term for "sin" in the New Testament Greek

is ἁμαρτία hamartia, which means failure, being in error, missing the mark.[4]

The Hebrew language has several other words for sin, each with its own specific meaning. The word pesha or "trespass" means a sin done out of rebelliousness. The word aveira means "transgression," and the word avone, or "iniquity," means a sin done out of moral failing.[5]

The following phrases: 'failure to do God's will,' 'missing the mark of what God requires of us,' "doing something wrong in the eyes of God,' 'rebellion towards God,' and 'moral failing' take longer to say than 'sin' but explain in greater detail what sin is to God, who is perfect.

A non-believer may listen more closely to what we are saying about Christianity if we use these phrases rather than the word 'sin,' and God's view of sinful actions will make more sense in today's world. The important information is that 'eternal death' (eternity without God) is still the result of unbelief and living in rebellion toward God.

For the wages of sin is death, but the free gift of God is eternal life in Christ Jesus our Lord (Romans 6:23).

'Satan' and 'devil' are words that can make non-believers laugh.

And no wonder, for even <u>Satan</u> disguises himself as an angel of light (2 Corinthians 11:14).

"The Hebrew word Satan means 'an adversary, one who resists.' While the activity of Satan is carried

---

4   https://en.wikipedia.org/wiki/Christian_views_on_sin
5   https://en.wikipedia.org/wiki/Jewish_views_on_sin

out in 'the world' (i.e., among those who do not acknowledge Christ as Lord) he also works against the followers of Christ" (Biblestudytools.com by Walter M. Dunnett).

"In the New Testament, the 'devil' becomes 'an evil principle or being standing against God'" (Biblestudytools.com by Walter M. Dunnett).

"An adversary of God and humankind" and "an evil being that is against God" are two good phrases we can use instead of "Satan" and "devil." Anyone should understand the thought of an evil being who is constantly trying to draw humankind away from God to their death by causing rebellious acts and refusing to do God's will.

Though we want to talk mostly about God's love and mercy, everyone needs to be aware of the consequences of their actions. God has provided a way to escape these consequences by sending His son to die for them. Believing that Jesus died and rose again to remove those consequences from us and by asking Jesus to forgive our sins will make us 'new creations' (a new person, a way to start over).

Whoever makes a practice of sinning is of the devil, for the devil has been sinning from the beginning. The reason the Son of God appeared was to destroy the works of the devil (1 John 3:8).

Submit yourselves therefore to God. Resist the devil, and he will flee from you (James 4:7).

And the great dragon was thrown down, that ancient serpent, who is called the devil and Satan, the deceiver of the whole world—he was thrown down to the earth, and his angels were thrown down with him (Revelation 12:9).

Think of Others

The reward for humility and fear of the LORD is riches and honor and life (Proverbs 22:4).

"It's all about you." Each of us should think these words every time we are dealing with another person. Instead, in today's world, "it's all about me" is the mindset of many. Most of the older generation were raised to think of other's wellbeing above their own, but generally, self-focus is now the norm.

How sad that each new generation believes more and more that their happiness and satisfaction are all-important. They have come to believe that if something feels good to them, benefits them, or brings them wealth and adoration, these things may be sought after without regard to another's feelings or welfare. They have been taught that they have a right to be happy.

Our rights in Christ are to be humble and to count others as more significant than ourselves. This does not make us weak. By no means. It makes us strong because we are not limited in seeking only our own way. We reach out and seek salvation and the joy of the Lord for others. We can build up and help those in need without worrying if our actions will take away from our own significance. When each person seeks the other person's happiness, everyone is happy.

Many of us were raised to believe that our happiness was not a right but a result of doing good for others. Today's world's messages are so confusing. We are told by friends that we have the right to be happy. Truly we know there is something wrong with this attitude of entitlement.

Everyone wants to be happy, but is that to be our sole goal in life? God promises joy through His Holy Spirit. Joy is eternal. Happiness is fleeting and true happiness comes from helping others and from giving of ourselves. Those who never experience giving without expecting something in return will never be truly happy.

We are seeing even in Christianity the gradual decline of putting other's interests and needs before self. The downtrend has been slow but steady and is the work of the deceiver. God gave His son to die for us, but we find it difficult to give of ourselves.

Every generation has both selfish people and giving people. Certainly, personality and upbringing play a large role in how we treat others. We all put ourselves first much of the time. We become too tired or too busy to do what would make someone else happy. Maybe we are a little bit angry at them and punish them by our actions. Maybe we just want what we want. How childish. This does not bring glory and honor to God.

There are hundreds or thousands of solar systems in the universe and none of them revolve around any one of us. And yet everything we do, think, or strive for is usually something that will benefit us. If our speech is full of "I, me and my" then we are probably not thinking of others before ourselves. It may not be our nature since the fall of man, but it is Christ's nature and we are new creatures in Christ. The old man must be kept under submission. Acts of giving bring happiness to everyone.

Remember the poor widow in the Bible who gave all that she had. Even though it was a very small amount, Jesus said that she gave more than anyone else because she gave out of her poverty. She gave from her heart, knowing that someone else would be blessed. When we give unselfishly, not only do we feel happy, but God blesses us in return.

Jesus looked up and saw the rich putting their gifts into the offering box, and he saw a poor widow put in two small copper coins. And he said, "Truly, I tell you, this poor widow has put in more than all of them. For they all contributed out of their abundance, but she out of her poverty put in all she had to live on" (Luke 21:1-4).

This is an example of truly thinking of others as more significant than ourselves and of true humility. This is God's will on earth and, in turn, makes us 'happy.'

Love one another with brotherly affection. Outdo one another in showing honor (Romans 12:10).

Ministers are Human

And I will give you shepherds after my own heart, who will feed you with knowledge and understanding (Jeremiah 3:15).

The ministers over our churches are human and not perfect but they are working to do God's will. It would be beneficial for us to remember that although we all minister to the world, we are not all called by God to preach His word and oversee His church. Overseeing a church is like being a CEO over a corporation. There is more to it than just preaching on Sunday mornings. God has willed these servants to carry out His work, and His will for us is to give them due respect.

Evangelists are people who seek to convert others to the Christian faith, especially by public preaching (usually outside the church). Shepherds and teachers work in the church educating the members and non-members about the scriptures.

Our church ministers or pastors are men and women who work tirelessly in a non-profit organization where they are required to know about finances, fundraising, counseling, teaching, children, youth, young adults, adults, and seniors. They perform weddings, baptisms, dedications, funerals and preach a message almost every week that must be interesting and engaging. They must work with a board of directors, worship team, and all the other staff. They are on call 24/7 and they must be nice and have a good sense of humor.

When they don't do things our way or don't smile brightly and call us by name as we leave the church, we complain. We complain about what they do, what they say, what they preach about, and how they treat or don't treat us.

However, when we are tempted to complain or feel what we consider righteous indignation, let us remember to keep our focus on what is God's will on earth and what He is doing, not what our minister is or is not doing. This is a temptation of the devil to bring division in the church and is definitely not God's will.

Obey your leaders and submit to them, for they are keeping watch over your souls, as those who will have to give an account. Let them do this with joy and not with groaning, for that would be of no advantage to you (Hebrews 13:17).

Ministers are just like us. They will fail. They will not feel equally about every aspect of the church or even every person. Some will feel passionate about children but not about missions or outreach. Some will put a lot of effort into teaching about the Bible but not so much on preaching messages about our daily lives. As humans, we all have things we are interested in and things we don't really care about. Ministers are the same.

We have days when things are going well and days when we feel down or tired. Ministers are the same. We worry about our families, finances, or car repairs. Ministers have the same issues, and yet we expect them to always be ready, willing and able to meet our needs. We expect them to listen to our complaints and have all the answers. We want their full attention when it is convenient for us.

We ask you, brothers, to respect those who labor among you and are over you in the Lord and admonish you, and to esteem them very highly in love because of their work. Be at peace among yourselves (1Thessalonians 5:12-13).

It is important to realize the increasing burdens being borne by our ministers and make sure we do not become one of those burdens. When we have a need, we should find a reasonable time to request counsel or aid. Mature Christians can give our ministers support and make sure that we are not taking their time away from young Christians who really need their attention.

When we disagree with something that is going on at the church or with a policy, we can bring that to a board member, deacon, or another leader. We don't always have to bring everything to the minister. Most importantly, we must always speak positively about our ministers to others so that we are not the cause of any division or gossip within the church by which some may fall away from God.

Not many of you should become teachers, my brothers, for you know that we who teach will be judged with greater strictness (James 3:1).

Ministers are held to higher standards than those of us in attendance. That is why they only become ministers if they truly feel that God has called them. If they are not called of God, they will surely fail and be miserable at the same time.

We can help our ministers by praying and encouraging

them. Be aware that the life that knocks us down can knock them down as well. They are human. They have personalities, likes and dislikes, and ideas that might not align with our own. But they are called of God, and His will is that we respect and esteem them and bring unity to the church. Let's do it.

Let the elders who rule well be considered worthy of double honor, especially those who labor in preaching and teaching (1 Timothy 5:17).

His Will for Us is Faith

Bless the L ORD, O you his angels, you mighty ones who do his word, obeying the voice of his word! (Psalm 103:20).

In Heaven, the angels obey God's will in all ways without question. God has asked us to do His will on earth as it is in Heaven; therefore, we must obey Him in all ways also. One of the ways we obey God is by having faith, which is a fruit of the Holy Spirit.

In all circumstances take up the shield of faith, with which you can extinguish all the flaming darts of the evil one (Ephesians 6:16).

Having faith in God in these troubling times is challenging. God does not test our faith, but our faith is often tested by this world. We know He CAN do anything, but true faith is about trusting that He WILL work on our behalf. Our faith is our shield against the evil one.

Count it all joy, my brothers, when you meet trials of various kinds, for you know that the testing of your faith produces steadfastness. And let steadfastness have its full effect, that you may be perfect and complete, lacking in nothing (James 1:2-4).

James instructs that we see the value of the trial, knowing with certainty that our God will strengthen us through it. It is not about God doing **our** will. It is about having faith that He will do what **needs** to be done and having confidence that we will survive it.

We rejoice because we have faith that God is working through the trial to bring about **His** plans.

We rejoice that we are being strengthened in our faith, becoming steadfast and ready for the next trial. We rejoice that we may be able to use what we are learning to help others. We rejoice because we know that the trial is temporary. We have many reasons to rejoice, but this takes obedience to God's will that we have faith.

And after you have suffered a little while, the God of all grace, who has called you to his eternal glory in Christ, will himself restore, confirm, strengthen, and establish you (1 Peter 5:10).

Faith as a belief in God and faith that God will bring us through trials are two different things. Believing in God and in His Son Jesus and asking Him to come into our hearts and forgive our sins is the first step in living the abundant life that Christ promised. This acceptance of Christ does not automatically produce the second kind of faith.

Faith is provided by God to accept Him and, following that, another faith is provided through His Holy Spirit to have confidence that He is working on our behalf with whatever this life throws at us.

The more we practice this second faith (trust, certainty, conviction) and the more we ask for this faith from God, the more we will be able to relax in times of trouble or uncertainty. We shouldn't rely on feelings to know that God is near, but when trials come, faith can settle our hearts and minds and take away fear and worry.

Many of us have heard the bamboo story, which supposedly illustrates persistence and not giving up, but there is another point to the story: faith.

A quick version of the story goes like this. There is a bamboo that must be watered constantly for five years before anything appears. Then in a matter of weeks, it grows to over 80 feet tall. Persistence in watering this plant is very important, but the person watering the plant must also have faith that it will eventually grow.

That faith is easy if you have seen it happen before, but the first time you plant the bamboo, faith would be very difficult and, after five long years, might falter. Once the bamboo grows, faith that it will happen again becomes easier. The more we see the results of our faith, the stronger our faith will become in the next trial.

When things are going well for us, our faith is not stretched. We may be thankful that things are smooth, or we may not go so far as to say we don't need God because all is well, but our faith does not grow during these times. Standing strong through a trial is the time our faith will either grow or die.

Faith is like working out at the gym. We work our faith muscles until they hurt but we see results, and because of that, our faith grows stronger. In this world we will have struggles more and more as the return of His Kingdom draws near. We need our faith to be strong. We need to be serious about our first kind of faith (belief) in God, and we need to practice and ask God to strengthen our second kind of faith (seriously knowing) that He is working for our good through all the difficulties of life.

Blessed is the man who remains steadfast under trial, for when he has stood the test he will receive the crown of life, which God has promised to those who love him (James 1:12).

Who is in Charge on Earth?

We know that we are from God, and the whole world lies in the power of the evil one (1 John 5:19).

As Christians, we belong to God. Christ is our Lord and King. His Holy Spirit leads and guides us and we follow His words. We walk with Him daily. When we have difficulty, we call to Him and He helps us. He teaches us and directs our paths. God's love is shown to us, and we know whom we worship. He oversees us, but we are not of this world, which lies in the power of the evil one.

There are many people who do not believe in God or follow Christ. They think they oversee their own destinies, that they are not ruled by God or anyone else. They are wrong. They are part of Satan's rebellion. Satan rules them.

And the great dragon was thrown down, that ancient serpent, who is called the devil and Satan, the deceiver of the whole world — he was thrown down to the earth, and his angels were thrown down with him (Revelation 12:9).

Satan was cast down to earth, and he has been leading his revolution against God ever since. His pride is so great that he makes himself equal with God, but he is not. He brings turmoil and unrest to the world and leads those who do not know God into disobedience,

Satan is a deceiver and an accuser of man, and he is doing everything possible to draw people into his rebellion against God, though most of his followers are unaware of their own obedience to him. Humanity does not realize that deciding

not to follow Christ is a decision **to** follow Satan.

In their case the god of this world has blinded the minds of the unbelievers, to keep them from seeing the light of the gospel of the glory of Christ, who is the image of God (2 Corinthians 4:4).

How then can God's will be done on earth? God has given humankind free will to decide whom we will serve. Satan leads astray those who do not accept Christ's gift of salvation. People follow him because they believe his lies, but he has only limited authority on earth because God is allowing it for a time. That time will come to an end. Come, Lord Jesus.

Jesus redeems those of us who accept Him and seeks out those who are still lost while we wait for the final judgment day when Satan will be banished once and for all. Christians have been delivered from Satan's limited authority; therefore, Christ works all things for our good because we love Him. We pray for God's Kingdom to come and for His will to be done on earth as it is in heaven. And we are the doers of His will on earth.

He has delivered us from the domain of darkness and transferred us to the kingdom of His beloved Son (Colossians 1:13).

Satan's rebellion is overtaking the world. We see it all around us. But he has no claim on the Christian. He knows his time is coming to an end soon and he is working overtime convincing the lost that sin will make them happy and give them a great life. He is not a ruler, he is not equal to God, but he is at work spreading disobedience and discord throughout the world.

Satan is a spirit at work in the world. He causes the world to see what is **right** (God's will) as **wrong** and what is **wrong** (sin) as **right**. The world is blind to truth and sin is considered righteous. Christians are mocked and those who do not understand God's great plan help spread Satan's lies.

And no wonder, for even Satan disguises himself as an angel of light (2 Corinthians 11:14).

We must remember that Satan uses whatever he can to keep people from Christ. His lies are not easily recognizable. Sometimes he uses good people to do good works on their own. Many good people are lost because they believe they don't need Christ. Those who achieve financial success often believe only in themselves and their money, and the world envies them.

Satan does not only use evil and hatred. He uses loneliness, pride, good works, relationships, jobs, politics, and even church to deceive people into believing they don't need God or that their works will save them. Christ came to destroy the works of the devil, and He does so through us. Praying for His will on earth is great but doing His will is better.

Be sober-minded; be watchful. Your adversary the devil prowls around like a roaring lion, seeking someone to devour (1 Peter 5:8).

Not only must we be watchful for ourselves, but we must understand what is happening in the world. We must understand Satan's ways of deception and protect ourselves from joining his rebellion against God even for a moment. Anything that disagrees with God's word, no matter how logical or righteous it may seem, is a lie of the spirit of darkness in the world.

We know who has charge of us, and we know who is deceiving the world. Our commission is to tell the good news, explain the deceptions, and bring people into the Kingdom of

God. We pray for His Kingdom to come at the final judgment and, while we wait, we are to do His will on earth. It is up to us to fight with all our strength against Satan's rebellion. We know Christ will win, but the question is, how many will be lost if we neglect to do His will?

> *Whoever makes a practice of sinning is of the devil, for the devil has been sinning from the beginning. The reason the Son of God appeared was to destroy the works of the devil (1 John 3:8).*

Justification of Our Will

> *So whoever knows the right thing to do and fails to do it, for him it is sin (James 4:17).*

The reverse of this scripture is also true. If we know that what we are doing is wrong and we do it anyway justifying it in our own minds it is still sin. Nowhere in scripture is sin justified by the words "except when you have a good reason" or "if you really want to."

We often leave church and become "normal" when we go to work or home, doing things of which God would not approve. We do little or big things that we know are wrong in God's eyes, but we say we did it for the right reason. We tend to try to justify our actions, but wrong is wrong and sin is sin. We cannot sin, e.g. steal or lie, sleep with a boyfriend or girlfriend for whatever reason and think that it is okay with God.

> *Draw near to God, and he will draw near to you. Cleanse your hands, you sinners, and purify your hearts, you double-minded (James 4:8).*

While we are in church, we would not think of committing a sin for any reason, but if once we exit the door, we begin to justify wrong actions with supposed 'right' reasons we are living in sin and are double-minded. This is not God's will.

We are splitting our lives into two distinct roles. One is our Christian role, and one is our worldly role. There are many split-life Christians justifying their sin, and this is not pleasing to God.

Everyone who makes a practice of sinning also practices lawlessness; sin is lawlessness (1 John 3:4).

Our human reasoning is not the same as God's. Sneaking onto private property to steal back a bicycle that had been stolen from us may seem fair, but it is sin. There are many legal ways to retrieve stolen property. Stealing is wrong no matter why we do it. Repaying evil with evil is sin. Stealing food to feed our families may seem right, but it is not, and God has another way if we only have faith.

Saying that we are doing the wrong things for the right reasons is lying to ourselves to justify our actions. It is just an excuse to do what is easy and what we want to do in the first place or what gives us a feeling of justice. We may fool ourselves. We may even fool others, but we do not fool God. We are sinning and in need of repentance and forgiveness.

He is a double-minded man, unstable in all his ways (James 1:8).

We cannot for one minute believe that sinning for a good reason is acceptable to God. We are to be the light in the world, but if the world sees Christians sinning, they won't look at the reasons behind the sin. They will judge us and mock us, and they will turn away from God because of our actions or words. They will call us hypocrites and deservedly so.

We must not have a split-life living one life as part of the world and the other life of service to God. If we are followers of God, then He should be our whole life. Everything we do should be subject to Him and His will.

I call heaven and earth to witness against you today, that I have set before you life and death, blessing and curse. Therefore choose life, that you and your offspring may live (Deuteronomy 30:19).

The Ripple Effect of God's Will

For my thoughts are not your thoughts, neither are your ways my ways, declares the Lord*. For as the heavens are higher than the earth, so are my ways higher than your ways and my thoughts than your thoughts (Isaiah 55:8-9).*

We try to impose our will on God. If He would just do things our way and in our timing, it would all work out better, faster and easier. We don't understand why things must be so difficult (for us).

God understands when we pray for things for ourselves, our families, and our friends. It is human nature. He gave us a brain, and we use it to come up with great ideas that can be used for His glory, but we are missing one important part.

We forget the ripple effect of God's will.

Trust in the Lord *with all your heart, and do not lean on your own understanding. In all your ways acknowledge him, and he will make straight your paths (Proverbs 3:5-6).*

God's ripple effect is like dropping a rock into a puddle. What affects us affects those around us, and what affects them affects those around them, and so on. We think our ideas would work out great (for us) and that might be true, but the ripple effect is what God sees.

He is always working in the lives of all His children to further His will that all come to know Him. This is amazing to think about. God is affecting all the people in all the world in ways that will draw them closer to Him every minute of every day.

If God were to provide something for us that we want but isn't right for us to have at the time, it might hurt another person (even without our knowledge) and that person might do something they shouldn't or perhaps turn away from God altogether. The ripple goes on and on. In a short time, hundreds of people will be affected by what we did of our own accord that wasn't what God wanted for us. Free will can get us into big trouble.

God sees all of it. He can see throughout our lifetimes the outcome of each action and reaction.

God gives us what we need, not what we want. When we make bad choices, He still works things out for good in the long run for those of us who love Him. It is impossible for us to comprehend how He can do this in a world of billions of people.

The next time we ask God for something and wonder why He doesn't do it our way, we should remember the number of people who are affected by one action. We are asking for something that will influence hundreds, and we don't even care. We are selfish children. We don't want God's will; we want ours.

God's plan is perfect. His timing is perfect, and even though we might struggle for a time, He is in control. It might be that what we are going through will have great positive consequences for others and help bring them to salvation. Most of us would give up a blessing if we knew for certain that someone would come into the Kingdom because of our sacrifice. We must have faith that God is working in every situation to bring about His will.

Give thanks in all circumstances; for this is the will of God in Christ Jesus for you (1 Thessalonians 5:18).

If God gave everyone what they want when they want it, which He could (He is God after all), both sports teams would win, no one would have to work, all lights would turn green during rush hour, and it would rain and be sunny and warm at the same time.

Let us remember to pray as the Lord taught us.

Your will be done, on earth as it is in heaven (Matthew 6:10).

God of All

For by him all things were created, in heaven and on earth, visible and invisible, whether thrones or dominions or rulers or authorities — all things were created through him and for him (Colossians 1:16).

Christians know that God created everything, including us, and that He loves us as His children.

When we come to the Lord and ask Him to forgive our sins and to come into our hearts, we know that we now have God's promises from His word. We also have His Holy Spirit, and we know that He is with us always. He is our God, King, Lord, and Father. And we are intelligent enough to know that others know our God also. We would be silly to think otherwise.

Know that the L<small>ORD</small>, he is God! It is he who made us, and we are his; we are his people, and the sheep of his pasture (Psalm 100:3).

We are blessed because of God's great love for us. He loves us so much that He sent His only son to die for our crimes to free us and to save us. What a magnificent God we love and serve. There is nothing that can separate us from God's love.

Yours, O Lord, is the greatness and the power and the glory and the victory and the majesty, for all that is in the heavens and in the earth is yours. Yours is the kingdom, O Lord, and you are exalted as head above all (1 Chronicles 29:11).

Yet, God is not the God of Christians only. Our God that saved us and lives in us is also the God of everyone else, even those who do not know Him. They may follow the devil and completely turn their backs on God even to the point of not believing He exists, but He is still God of all. He created them and He loves them.

He continues to stand next to them and knock on their heart's door, loving them and wanting them to answer His call. He is even God of the people we don't like, such as sinners, the hateful, murderers, those who belong to other religions, and those who hate Christians. He is still their God whether they know it or not. But we must know it, and we must love them because He is the God of all.

Behold, to the Lord your God belong heaven and the heaven of heavens, the earth with all that is in it (Deuteronomy 10:14).

We often hear that, in our behavior and in our attitude and words, non-believers will see God. Seeing His love in us may be the only time they see what God can do in their lives. They may ignore what God is doing all around them, but they will either see God in us or they will see how we fail Him.

If we fail to show Him in our lives, they may continue in

their unbelief. We belong to Him, and we represent Him. We are not required to show Him only to those who already believe, but to all His children.

Sometimes in our desire to serve God and do what is 'right,' we turn away from sinners. God's word does instruct us not to marry an unbeliever. It tells us that hanging out with bad company will ruin our morals, and it tells us not to associate with other **believers** who continue to sin and not to take part in sin. But He also tells us to love our neighbors as ourselves. He does not tell us to turn away and ignore sharing the good news with these people.

> *Do not be unequally yoked with unbelievers. For what partnership has righteousness with lawlessness? Or what fellowship has light with darkness? (2 Corinthians 6:14).*
>
> *Do not be deceived: "Bad company ruins good morals" (1 Corinthians 15:33).*
>
> *But now I am writing to you not to associate with anyone who bears the name of brother if he is guilty of sexual immorality or greed, or is an idolater, reviler, drunkard, or swindler — not even to eat with such a one (1 Corinthians 5:11).*
>
> *Take no part in the unfruitful works of darkness, but instead expose them (Ephesians 5:11).*

We are to spread the gospel to all the world. But thinking we are doing right, we turn away from the homosexuals, the abusers, the murderers, and thieves. We turn away from the Muslims, the drunkards, the homeless, felons, and the mentally ill. These are human beings that were created by God. These are people He loves and, in whose lives, He continues to work for His glory (hopefully through us).

> *So whatever you wish that others would do to you, do also to them, for this is the Law and the Prophets (Matthew 7:12).*

Some of us have been saved out of lives like those mentioned, and some of us have been blessed to have lives that were relatively easy. Somewhere along the line, we chose to follow God. Others also need this opportunity, and we need to provide it.

Though it is difficult for us to love those of different lifestyles, especially those who hate us, we should remember that they have a void in their hearts that can only be filled by God because He created them. Help them recognize their father among the multitude of false gods out there. If we never knew our father, how could we recognize Him? Someone (we) must introduce Him. We cannot introduce Him if we are avoiding His lost children. We must be brave in doing God's will on earth.

> *For we do not wrestle against flesh and blood, but against the rulers, against the authorities, against the cosmic powers over this present darkness, against the spiritual forces of evil in the heavenly places (Ephesians 6:12).*

The Question of Submission

> *Wives submit to your own husbands, as to the Lord. For the husband is the head of the wife <u>even as Christ is the head of the church</u>, his body, and is himself its Savior. <u>Now as the church submits to Christ, so also wives should submit in everything to their husbands</u>.*

Husbands, love your wives, as Christ loved the church and gave himself up for her, that he might sanctify her, having cleansed her by the washing of water with the word (Ephesians 5:22-26).

God's will on earth regarding everything humankind should do and say is explained in His word. Christians try to follow and do His will on earth as best we know how. However, interpretation of His word often does not consider who was writing, who was being written to, and what was going on at the time it was written. This is called taking scripture out of context. Context is very important. Though God's word never changes, we must be wise and in prayer when reading it, asking for the Holy Spirit's guidance.

There are Bible verses instructing women to submit to their husbands in everything. Does this mean that women are not equal to men? Of course not. Women are equal children of God, are given gifts from Him, are led into ministry, and have wisdom and many other wonderful traits.

Many women in the New Testament led churches and taught the Good News to others. Women are called of God to be ministers of the Gospel just as men are. This topic of submission is very difficult for both men and women to understand and can cause great difficulty in marriages and churches.

The Bible's word for 'Submit' is hupakouó: <u>to listen, attend to</u> Original Word: ὑπακούω Part of Speech: Verb Transliteration: hupakouó Phonetic Spelling: (hoop-ak-oo'-o) Definition: <u>to listen, attend to</u> (Strong's Concordance).

We can see in Strong's definition that when women are told to be submissive to their husbands, they are being told to listen to them and attend to their ideas and opinions. This is not a matter of who gets the remote control. It's all about

God's will.

Another word we need to understand is **'everything'**. The Greek word in the Bible is 'Pas,' which means **all** in the sense of each part that applies. Looking at the writings to the church we can see that *Pas* is related to the church and therefore concerning spiritual matters or each part that applies.

Pás ("each, every") means "all" in the sense of "each (every) part that applies." The emphasis of the total picture then is on "one piece at a time." (ananeóō) then focuses on the part(s) making up the whole – viewing the whole in terms of the individual parts.

The apostle's letters, which are most of the scriptures we read, are written to the churches and concern specific church matters. To take one sentence out of a letter and base our behavior on that one sentence is not right, and we cannot pull out only those scriptures that support our ideas.

But I want you to understand that the head of every man is Christ, the head of a wife is her husband, and the head of Christ is God (1 Corinthians 11:3).

As every organization has a head, God desires the man to be the head of the household as Christ is the head of the man. This does not mean that there will always be agreement between the husband and wife or that the wife must be in an attitude of servitude. Someone must have the final word if that word agrees with God's word.

Each person in a marriage has different strengths, experiences, and knowledge that help the family unit when making decisions. Each should be listened to and attention given to their specific wisdom. In many instances, the wife will have the final say because of her expertise. This shows wisdom and leadership on the part of the husband.

All Scripture is breathed out by God and profitable for teaching, for reproof, for correction, and for training in righteousness (2 Timothy 3:16).

We are all one in Christ. We are the church body submitting to and listening to Christ. His word is profitable to us. His word educates us and leads us into right decisions. The words of husbands who prayerfully study God's word and use wisdom in their homes will profit the entire family as will those of the wife.

Love is patient and kind; love does not envy or boast; it is not arrogant or rude. It does not insist on its own way; it is not irritable or resentful; it does not rejoice at wrongdoing but rejoices with the truth. Love bears all things, believes all things, hopes all things, endures all things (1 Corinthians 13:4-7).

God's Plans – Thy Will

The heart of man plans his way, but the LORD *establishes his steps (Proverbs 16:9).*

We would all like to know God's plan for our lives and for specific times within our lives. He seldom does things the way we would do them, but we trust that He has plans that are for our benefit.

When we look back on our lives, we can see where His plans were obviously better than what we had asked for in the first place. We can also see times we went ahead with our own plans only to mess things up. Nevertheless, God rescued us and made a good outcome of our bad choices when we followed His leading.

Many are the plans in the mind of a man, but it is the

purpose of the LORD that will stand (Proverbs 19:21).

God's word is full of wisdom concerning His plans. One thing we know for certain is that He wants everyone to come to know Him, to accept His son's sacrifice, and to be forgiven of their sins. All other plans lead to this one. Salvation of His creation is the center plan toward which all others work.

Redemption for all is the purpose of the Lord. We should look at our ideas about how things should go with His purpose in mind. Is what we are asking for in line with the overall plan of God? Our faith in God and in His Son Jesus saved us, and now that faith must sustain us during difficult times when we wish we knew His plan. We must take one day at a time, trusting that as we walk, He is with us leading, guiding, and protecting us from harm.

For by grace you have been saved through faith. And this is not your own doing; it is the gift of God, not a result of works, so that no one may boast (Ephesians 2:8-9).

Though we believe we know best in many situations and that doing things our way could not possibly do any harm, God's will is always best. We often find ourselves praying, "God, just make my idea your will. It will work and it will be perfect." The attitude to do our own thing is self-centered, not God-centered, and we all do it.

Once we have salvation through Christ, we can be led by His Holy Spirit to do His will. If His plan is our focus, our plans will align with His. Looking back at the times we have asked God for *our* will, but He gave us *His* will, we can see how much better His will was in the end.

For we are his workmanship, created in Christ Jesus for good works, which God prepared beforehand, that we should walk in them (Ephesians 2:10).

God prepared everything beforehand to work out His perfect plan. It is our free will that causes problems. Praise God that His great love for us makes His will benefit us in the long run. Each singular event in our lives is just a blip on the screen of eternity. It may seem all-important to us at the time but it will pass, and if we allow God to have His way, it will bring Him glory and it will bring us peace.

> *For I know the plans I have for you, declares the* Lord, *plans for welfare and not for evil, to give you a future and a hope. Then you will call upon me and come and pray to me, and I will hear you. You will seek me and find me, when you seek me with all your heart. I will be found by you, declares the* Lord, *and I will restore your fortunes and gather you from all the nations and all the places where I have driven you, declares the* Lord, *and I will bring you back to the place from which I sent you into exile (Jeremiah 29:11-14).*

As we learn more about God and draw closer in our personal relationship with Him, our trust in Him will grow. We will ask for His will and mean it. We may still throw in a few hints about what we would like to see happen (because we can't help ourselves), but we will know that He has the best outcome for us in His plan.

> *"Before I formed you in the womb I knew you, and before you were born I consecrated you; I appointed you a prophet to the nations" (Jeremiah 1:5).*

Thy Will or My Will

> *Therefore do not be foolish, but understand what the will of the Lord is (Ephesians 5:17).*

When Christ taught His disciples and us to pray in what we call the Lord's Prayer, one part was for God's will to be done on earth as it is done in heaven. What we are praying for is God's ultimate will or desire that none should perish. His will is that everyone accepts Him, loves Him, and follows Him. To that end, He is constantly working on the hearts of humankind.

The Lord is not slow to fulfill his promise as some count slowness, but is patient toward you, not wishing that any should perish, but that all should reach repentance (2 Peter 3:9).

Who desires all people to be saved and to come to the knowledge of the truth (1 Timothy 2:4).

To accomplish His will, God uses us, so when we pray for His will to be done, we are praying for His will with us so that we can be used for His purpose. We are praying that we can go forth and bring about change in this world. He uses us to reach out to those who need Him and to show the way to salvation. We are part of bringing His will to earth. We are praying for ourselves to be willing and available for His use.

Go therefore and make disciples of all nations, baptizing them in the name of the Father and of the Son and of the Holy Spirit (Matthew 28:19).

To be responsible for bringing about God's will on earth is a serious calling, and we have free will to ignore that responsibility and live out our Christian lives for ourselves alone. But how can God's will be done on earth if we who know and love Him don't help to bring it about?

We can choose our path. We can enjoy God's great blessings in our own lives, knowing that we have been saved and will spend eternity with Him. We can be satisfied, but to sincerely pray for His will to be done on earth requires more from us.

> *For this is the will of God, that by doing good you should put to silence the ignorance of foolish people (1 Peter 2:15).*

Not only does God's will on earth mean reaching out to everyone else, but God also has a will for each of us personally, and for that, we also pray. Daily He leads and guides us in our own lives. There is a multitude of scriptures about God's will for us as individuals. Many concern sins and what to avoid, how to live, and how to treat others. The Bible instructs us about God's will for our faith, how to be strong in the face of struggles, and what to watch out for that may cause us to sin.

Living in God's will for our own lives also helps to bring about His will for others. God will not force His will on anyone but will gently guide and direct our path as we allow. It is up to us to listen and to follow so that we will know His will on earth and do it.

> *Do not be conformed to this world, but be transformed by the renewal of your mind, that by testing you may discern what is the will of God, what is good and acceptable and perfect (Romans 12:2).*

God's will for our individual lives is beautiful and full of blessings. The Bible tells us how to live God's will each day. Anything we might struggle with is addressed in the Bible, and we can learn His will in every situation by prayer and by reading or hearing God's word.

> *All Scripture is breathed out by God and profitable for teaching, for reproof, for correction, and for training in righteousness, that the man of God may be competent, equipped for every good work (2 Timothy 3:16-17).*

The grass withers, the flower fades, but the word of our God will stand forever (Isaiah 40:8).

When we pray in the Lord's prayer God's will for ourselves and His will for His creation to be accomplished on earth, we are asking for a powerful move of the Holy Spirit. We are asking for everyone to come to salvation through Christ. We are asking for help and strength as we go forth through everything the world throws at us.

We tend to skim over that short sentence in the Lord's Prayer because it seems so simple. We need to realize that we are partners with God in bringing about His will on earth and be committed to doing His work with all the power of the Holy Spirit at work within us.

Now to him who is able to do far more abundantly than all that we ask or think, according to the power at work within us, to him be glory in the church and in Christ Jesus throughout all generations, forever and ever. Amen (Ephesians 3:20-21).

Chapter Six

Give Us this Day our Daily Bread

No need to worry. God's got this!

Therefore do not be anxious, saying, 'What shall we eat?' or 'What shall we drink?' or 'What shall we wear?' For the Gentiles seek after all these things, and your heavenly Father knows that you need them all (Matthew 6:31-32).

Worry is a common state of being, even among Christians. In our daily lives, we are bombarded with things to worry about. We worry about others and how they are doing. We worry about our children, our responsibilities at work and at church. We worry about the world and politics, how we should respond on Facebook, and we worry about money. These are legitimate concerns, so we worry about them. How can we not?

Being constantly in a state of worry or concern over the

things that God has promised to provide is like working at your job but not sure you will get a paycheck. Worry is not healthy and does not fill us with the joy of the Lord. We know this but it seems out of our control. Why is God's promise of less value than the promise of a paycheck at the end of our work period?

Only with help from the Holy Spirit can our trust and faith in God grow stronger and our worry transform into a calm assurance that all will be well. Only by prayer and asking for more faith can we be at peace when we would normally fret. Only by being still and knowing that our God can do all things can we have that assurance.

Stopping thoughts in the midst of worry takes being alert and mindful of the times when worry takes control. Reading God's word, a Christian book, listening to Christian music, or a preacher can take our minds off worry and onto God's love and grace. The Holy Spirit will help train us to stop the negative thoughts and replace them with the sure knowledge that God will take care of us.

And my God will supply every need of yours according to his riches in glory in Christ Jesus (Philippians 4:19).

We agree that God knows exactly what we need. He knows when we need material things, and He knows when it is best for us not to have those things. When His answer to our prayers is 'no,' that is what we need.

God will meet our needs according to His riches in glory. God's riches are not like our riches. His riches are love, joy, peace, patience, kindness, goodness, gentleness, faithfulness, and self-control. Yes, He meets our financial and physical needs (not wants) but His goals are not our goals. His goal is for us to have a close personal relationship with Him, trusting that what He provides will be sufficient and we will be able to do His work.

And God is able to make all grace abound to you, so that having all sufficiency in all things at all times, you may abound in every good work (2 Corinthians 9:8).

When God meets our needs, His intention is for us to abound in every good work. We are His representatives here, and our lives, our trust, and our faith need to show the world that He provides for us even when He says 'no' or 'not yet.' Unbelievers and new Christians need to see the peace that He gives to us because we believe (we know) that He loves us and will provide.

He is the almighty God and can do anything He wants, but what He wants is for us to have a stronger relationship with Him. He wants us to show the world who He is so that they will come to Him. He will meet our needs (not wants) to accomplish His goal.

If we are anxious and fretting about every little thing, it will show to those around us. Remember the ripple effect that our actions and attitudes cause. The world is watching and will have no reason to turn to God in their time of need if we can't trust Him in ours.

Those who do not come to God will not have this peace. They may work hard, and their physical needs may or may not be met, but the abundant life God provides inside our hearts and minds is not theirs. Our treasure is in heaven, and our treasure is in our relationship with God, not in what we are worrying about here.

Walking with God is the journey of a lifetime, and He has promised to meet our needs if we follow Him and take steps of faith. It is a wonderful trip as we learn to trust in Him. No need to worry. God's got this!

Contentment is Great Gain

But Godliness with contentment is great gain, for we brought nothing into the world, and we cannot take anything out of the world. But if we have food and clothing, with these we will be content (1 Timothy 6:6-8).

Striving, stressing, worrying, and working are driving the world into a frenzy of discontentment. In 1 Timothy, contentment is considered to be great gain. God desires this for us and for our walk with Him. If we can know contentment in all situations, we will truly gain His abundant life.

The world is not living abundantly and we who spend our time in worry are not living abundantly either. Stress and worry cause us to make bad choices, react badly to situations, and cause hurt in our relationships. We have accepted the world's offering of being discontent, believing that only by never being satisfied will we accomplish anything in life. This is the opposite of God's idea of gain.

Contentment or even settling for less than what we really want is not laziness, though the world may say so. Some may view those who are content as lacking motivation or energy, especially those who don't have as much as the world believes adequate. But even those with abundance are not content as they continue to seek more and more.

The apostle Paul was far from lazy. He made tents and worked to support himself so that he was not a burden to the churches. He traveled from town to town preaching the gospel. He wrote letters, was beaten, ended up in prison, almost drowned, almost starved, and was eventually beheaded. However, he was content in every situation.

The truth about contentment is that no matter what we have or don't have, being content is the true prize. If we are content, then whatever we have or whatever we are doing is enough.

Contentment is worth more than gold. If we love God and make choices based on His word, our situation will always be what it is supposed to be, and we can be content knowing we are held in His loving arms.

> ***For the sake of Christ, then, I am content with weaknesses, insults, hardships, persecutions, and calamities. For when I am weak, then I am strong (2 Corinthians 12:10).***

Contentment is trusting in God that all our needs (not wants) will be met by Him. Paul knew that God would take care of him. When we are content, we are defeating our stress. We are defeating worry. We are defeating the devil trying to make us think that the worst is happening and we aren't going to make it through. Contentment is faith.

Knowing that God's word says He will meet our needs should empower us to enjoy contentment every day, no matter what is happening. This is not a weakness and does not mean we are throwing up our hands and giving in. It means we are certain that our God will work in our situation for the good of all.

It is paramount for us to show true contentment to the world. We need to show our great trust in God, that He is always with us, and that we are certain He is working in our lives even when we are struggling. Being content with our current circumstances is unfathomable to the world. What a wonderful way to show them what a great God and Father we have.

Unbelievers and those who have not attained contentment will continue in stress and worry. They will not understand our calmness in catastrophe or our satisfaction with less than the world says will make us happy. Our contentment will confuse them and that is good. Our contentment is an opening to proclaim the Good News of Christ to the lost.

We can be at peace. We have contentment offered to us just by knowing that Christ has forgiven our sins and is with us all the time. Contentment is gain, and knowing where we will spend eternity is contentment enough.

> ***You keep him in perfect peace whose mind is stayed on you, because he trusts in you (Isaiah 26:3).***

His Promises are True

> ***"...not one word has failed of all the good things that the LORD your God promised concerning you. All have come to pass for you; not one of them has failed" (Joshua 23:14).***

Daily, our goal should be to build up our faith and relationship with our Heavenly Father. We battle the enemy, making our way through this world's evil muck and quicksand, to God's light on the other side. Knowing that God has promised to be with us to guide us and to strengthen us makes these struggles easier. We must hold onto His promises if we want to be successful in this battle.

Christ instructed us to ask for our daily bread when we pray, which means our needs for that day, and He promised to meet those needs. But there is so much more that is promised to us. There are 5,467 promises from God in the Bible for us, our families, our lives, and our eternity.

The promises in the Old Testament pertaining to the coming of Christ have all been fulfilled. Each prophecy and each statement concerning His death and resurrection have come to pass. We can believe God's word and trust that He will keep His promises not only because we love Him, but because He has proven that He is faithful.

No, I will not break my covenant; I will not take back a single word I said (Psalm 89:34 NLT).

Remembering past promises that God has kept in our own lives builds our faith in His promises for each new day. We hold on to these promises to strengthen and encourage us as the enemy throws in our way lie after lie and problem after problem to distract us from trusting that God will provide our daily bread. We should look back at what we have come through, knowing that it was God who worked it out.

And my God will supply every need of yours according to his riches in glory in Christ Jesus (Philippians 4:19).

God has promised to provide our daily bread (our daily needs). What else has He promised? What else is helpful to us in life? He has promised that if we accept Him and ask for forgiveness of our sins, He will forgive us. He will give us a new heart and eternal life.

And this is the promise that he made to us — eternal life (1 John 2:25).

He has promised us a new heart.

And I will give you a new heart, and a new spirit I will put within you. And I will remove the heart of stone from your flesh and give you a heart of flesh (Ezekiel 36:26).

He has promised that we will be cleansed and made new.

If we confess our sins, he is faithful and just to forgive us our sins and to cleanse us from all unrighteousness (1 John 1:9).

He has promised that our sins will be removed from us, that they will be buried, and that He will not remember them.

These are the promises that we hold onto when Satan the accuser throws our past mistakes into our faces and tell us we are not worthy of God's love and forgiveness.

God has promised to be with us every second of every day and to give us the wisdom we need to navigate life and resist temptations. He will strengthen us and hold us up, giving us what we need in every situation if we will just call on His name.

If any of you lacks wisdom, let him ask God, who gives generously to all without reproach, and it will be given him (James 1:5).

We forget that God is standing ready to provide whatever we need to win this battle. In this world, we will have trouble and heartache. We will struggle and suffer loss. This is the world we live in and it is under the control of the powers of darkness until Christ's return. But Christians are not of this world. We belong to Christ, and we have His promises to keep us from giving in to the world's evil.

No temptation has overtaken you that is not common to man. God is faithful, and he will not let you be tempted beyond your ability, but with the temptation he will also provide the way of escape, that you may be able to endure it (1 Corinthians 10:13).

We have the ability today to use our computers, tablets, Siri, Alexa, cell phones, and Google to get information about anything. Use these tools to find God's promises that will encourage each other during difficult times.

Fear not, for I am with you; be not dismayed, for I am your God; I will strengthen you, I will help you, I will uphold you with my righteous right hand (Isaiah 41:10).

There are promises about finances, marriage, employment, health, children, peace, temptation, fear, pain, and more. We do not have to walk unaware through our maze of difficulties. God has provided ways for us to live this life abundantly with His promises. This is our daily bread. His promises are true.

Fully convinced that God was able to do what he had promised (Romans 4:21).

There is Hope for Today

For whatever was written in former days was written for our instruction, that through endurance and through the encouragement of the Scriptures we might have hope (Romans 15:4).

As mentioned in Chapter 4, 'hope' is a sure confidence that what we hope for will come to pass. Today, we use the word 'hope' for things we want to happen but that we don't feel confident about. The definition and use of the word 'hope' have changed from how it was used in biblical times.

Today, we say, 'I hope this or that' or 'I hope I sleep well tonight' and often the word 'so' follows, as in 'I hope so,' but this use of the word 'hope' implies that it might <u>not</u> happen. There is **doubt** in the way we use 'hope' today. It is no wonder that reading about 'hope' in God does not have the impact on us that it should.

When we read scripture about hope, it means a **certainty** because we know God is faithful and what He has promised He will do. We are to rejoice in our hope. The Scriptures would not encourage us to have hope if there was any doubt about our hope.

How can we rejoice in hope if there is doubt attached to it? We have all heard the phrase 'there is no doubt about it.' This is Biblical hope. There is assurance in Biblical hope. There is faith.

Rejoice in hope, be patient in tribulation, be constant in prayer (Romans 12:12).

As Christians, we have hope (the assurance or promise) for eternal life with Christ and we rejoice in it but there is also hope for each of us today. We have hope that Christ will be with us. We have hope that He is guiding our path and providing our daily needs. We know these things are true.

Unfortunately, we are a doubting people. There is a limit to our confidence in what we hope for even if what we hope for comes from God. We have been let down by ourselves and others so that our faith and our hope are not the confident assurances they should be. We must choose to believe God's word and change our view of the hope we read about in the Bible.

Since we have been raised using the wrong meaning for 'hope,' it is difficult to change, but when we say that our hope is in the Lord, we have the assurance that eternal life with Him is ours.

What we struggle with is having the same assurance that He will take care of us here and now. But we **can** walk through each day with confidence with an all-powerful God beside us. He cares about daily things, not just eternal things.

Now faith is the assurance of things hoped for, the conviction of things not seen (Hebrews 11:1).

We **want** so much more than we **need,** and we confuse our wants with needs. When our wants are not provided, our worldly hope is infused with doubt. However, we must remember and instill in ourselves with the help of the Holy Spirit that God is faithful. He is meeting our needs. He will always meet our needs if we have faith and hope in Him.

"And now, O Lord, for what do I wait? My hope is in you (Psalm 39:7).

Unmet Expectations

The hope of the righteous brings joy, but the expectation of the wicked will perish (Proverbs 10:28).

God gives us what we need, not necessarily what we want. God answers our prayers. He even answers when we don't pray, but sometimes His answers are not what we expect. Christians know that it is better to receive what God wants for us than what we want for ourselves, but it is still difficult to want and expect a certain result and to have that expectation unmet.

Having expectations can be fun. Looking forward to a raise or promotion, a perfect score, or a special gift can be exhilarating. However, when those expectations don't come to pass, they can lead to frustration and even anger and depression. When we request something from God and are sure that He will provide it, but it doesn't come in a way or time that we expect, we may lose faith or feel that God does not love us. Therefore, Christ taught us to ask for our daily bread. He did not add a bunch of wants and desires to the Lord's Prayer. Daily bread is basic and easy to understand. We should be asking for what will be essential for the day, and we can expect that need to be met.

Rejoice in hope, be patient in tribulation, be constant in prayer (Romans 12:12).

Constantly expecting things to be as we want them ends up making life a roller coaster ride full of extreme highs and very low lows. It is not a victorious Christian life to always being in a state of expectation or despair over something that did or didn't come to pass. And yet, never having any expectations can also be depressing. That is why we bring our requests to God but trust that His way of answering will be best.

It is a dilemma. Humans have many expectations, whether they are expected answers to prayer or expectations of our jobs, families, or goals in life. For Christians, it is better to have hope than expectations. In scripture, according to both the Hebrew and the Greek, 'hope' is a strong and confident expectation. This implies a certainty that when our hope is in God, He will do as He has promised.[6]

May the God of hope fill you with all joy and peace in believing, so that by the power of the Holy Spirit you may abound in hope (Romans 15:13).

God will provide our daily bread when we need it and how we need it based on His promises. The fruit of the Holy Spirit that God has offered us are love, joy, peace, patience, kindness, goodness, faithfulness, gentleness, and self-control. These things we can always ask for and confidently expect.

The fruit of not getting what we want is anger, frustration, competitiveness, detachment, loneliness, pessimism, resentment, stubbornness, and suffering. These come from having expectations that are unmet and usually undeserved, unrealistic, or prideful. Expectation is not the same as *hope* as the Bible defines it.

"And now, O Lord, for what do I wait? My hope is in you" (Psalm 39:7).

Our Heavenly Father wants us to bring our requests before

---

[6] Jennifer Chamberlain, "Fresh Fruit: Meditations on the Fruit of the Holy Spirit" Dove Christian Publishers, 2018.

Him. He wants us to ask for our daily bread, not bread for a week or month or year. He does not mind if we cry out to Him with desires, even those we know may not be what He wants for us. He loves us and He will answer as any loving father would. He will give us what we need. If we run ahead and do things our own way, He is ready and willing to help bring us back into fellowship and make good things come to those who love Him.

Chapter Seven

And Forgive Us Our Trespasses/Debts as We Forgive Those Who Trespass Against Us

Lies and Half-truths

Therefore, having put away falsehood, let each one of you speak the truth with his neighbor, for we are members one of another (Ephesians 4:25).

Christ forgives our trespasses, and there are so many. For example, we lie. We tell half-truths. We might think of it as self-preservation. Maybe we have done something we shouldn't have and need to make up an excuse. Maybe we believe it is better to say we didn't do it at all. "It wasn't me."

We might think we are protecting someone or trying not to hurt them. We may just be taking a sick day from work without being sick.

Unless we are lying to save a life, it seems that Christians should be able to find ways to say no, disagree, take time off from work, not go to church or a gathering without resorting to half-truth storytelling. Honesty takes practice and might even seem blunt or off-putting to some, but Christ always told the truth or kept His mouth shut. Sometimes staying silent is the best way to go.

If we often lie and are caught in our lies our witness for the Lord will be destroyed. People will not believe anything that comes from us, even if it is true. Lost trust is difficult to recover.

> ***Lying lips are an abomination to the Lord, but those who act faithfully are his delight (Proverbs 12:22).***

From childhood, telling falsehoods has seemed like second nature. "Who broke that lamp?" "I don't know." Our natural state from birth into this sinful world is one of not wanting to be blamed for something bad. We want to avoid punishment and embarrassment so we cover our actions with something that makes us look better.

Lying to excuse ourselves or justify our actions to get out of doing something that makes us uncomfortable is a sin. Lies are selfishly motivated. They are intended to make things easier for the liar. Making ourselves the center of our focus leads to a multitude of lies. Making God the center leads to thinking of others first and treating them the way we want to be treated. We would prefer to have the truth, so we should tell the truth.

> ***There are six things that the Lord hates, seven that are an abomination to him: haughty eyes, a lying tongue,***

and hands that shed innocent blood, a heart that devises wicked plans, feet that make haste to run to evil, a false witness who breathes out lies, and one who sows discord among brothers (Proverbs 6:16-19).

The Lord hates lying, and it is listed in Proverbs 6 twice: once as lying words in general and once as bearing false witness or telling a lie about someone else or spreading rumors and gossip and creating chaos and drama. There are those who seem to enjoy pitting people against each other with half-truths and lies. Avoid these people, ignore what they say about others, and never spread their gossip.

Show each other and non-believers the importance of speaking the truth. Even when it feels good to be included in the group that supposedly knows the inside scoop, we must test the intention and the spirit of the speaker against what we know God wants and refuse to give the devil a foothold.

God investigates our hearts to see what is central to us. We cannot fool Him. Telling God that our lies were just little and were necessary to make life run smoothly or to help someone in need doesn't convince Him. We are lying to God.

Do not lie to one another, seeing that you have put off the old self with its practices and have put on the new self, which is being renewed in knowledge after the image of its creator (Colossians 3:9-10).

When we were forgiven for our sins of the past, we were made new, and yet we continue to sin because no one is perfect. We must strive with the help of the Holy Spirit to be the new creation God made us and keep the old one down, seeking forgiveness daily. Being renewed in knowledge by what we put into our minds, namely God's word, will help us grow closer and become more like Christ, which is the goal. Then we will be shown ways to be truthful, and God will bless us.

> *For nothing is hidden that will not be made manifest, nor is anything secret that will not be known and come to light (Luke 8:17).*

The Measure We Use

> *"Judge not, that you be not judged. For with the judgment you pronounce you will be judged, and with the measure you use it will be measured to you. Why do you see the speck that is in your brother's eye, but do not notice the log that is in your own eye? Or how can you say to your brother, 'Let me take the speck out of your eye,' when there is the log in your own eye? You hypocrite first take the log out of your own eye, and then you will see clearly to take the speck out of your brother's eye" (Matthew 7:1-29).*

We know this verse well "judge not, that you be not judged." Unfortunately, we do not try to understand the end of the next sentence, "For with the judgment you pronounce you will be judged **and with the measure you use it will be measured to you.**"

When we measure people, we use our past experiences, our own failures, or times we have been duped or conned. The more people let us down, the harsher our measurement of the next person to come along. This is not what Jesus did.

Our Lord was treated badly, lied to, tested, scorned, and judged. People called him a liar and a blasphemer, a con artist of the day. But Christ, when meeting and dealing with people who had done terrible things and would most likely have done them again without His love, forgave them and loved them. He measured them not by their past but by what

God made them to be.

God forgives us our past and present mistakes, and He continues to love us. He gave and continues to give everyone chance after chance to come to Him and to change their lives. Who are we to measure others by their past or even their present? The measure we use will be how we are also measured in the end. Some that we meet may not end up being our best friends, but they deserve to be measured according to God's measurement, not ours.

> *Therefore, you have no excuse, O man, every one of you who judges. For in passing judgment on another you condemn yourself, because you, the judge, practice the very same things. We know that the judgment of God rightly falls on those who practice such things. Do you suppose, O man—you who judge those who practice such things and yet do them yourself—that you will escape the judgment of God? Or do you presume on the riches of his kindness and forbearance and patience, not knowing that God's kindness is meant to lead you to repentance? But because of your hard and impenitent heart you are storing up wrath for yourself on the day of wrath when God's righteous judgment will be revealed (Romans 2:1-5).*

Let us be blunt with ourselves. Sometimes we are doing things we shouldn't and judging the person next to us for doing what they shouldn't be doing. What truly matters is that we do what God has called us to do in our hearts. As Christ gives many chances to those who struggle but sincerely desire to change, let us give many chances also.

We cannot give up on people because we are measuring them with our measurements, and they are falling short. It is about their salvation, and whatever we can do to bring them into the family of God is what we must do. No measurement is necessary. Only God knows the whole story of how a person became whom they are.

> *Why do you pass judgment on your brother? Or you, why do you despise your brother? For we will all stand before the judgment seat of God (Romans 14:10).*

Give of ourselves even to those who may not "measure up" to our standards. We are not wise. We need God to lead our hearts. When God measures us, let Him find that we have measured others rightly.

> *Live in harmony with one another. Do not be haughty, but associate with the lowly. Never be wise in your own sight (Romans 12:16).*

The World is Watching

> *So whoever knows the right thing to do and fails to do it, for him it is sin (James 4:17).*

This verse, that I refer to many times, infers that Christians (we know the right things to do from God's word) sin when we fail to do what is right. But there are times when we may unconsciously do the wrong thing in haste and without forethought, especially when our relationship with God is new. It is not His will that we continue to be blind to our own mistakes. His Holy Spirit will make us aware through our conscience because we are His voice in the world, and the world is watching us.

The Greek translation of the Aramaic word for trespass as used in the Lord's Prayer is Paráptōma, and means to fall away after being close-beside, i.e. a *lapse* (deviation) from the truth; an error, "slip up"; wrongdoing that can be (relatively) unconscious, "non-deliberate." **(Strong's Original Greek).**

And Forgive Us Our Trespasses/Debts

We know that slip-ups happen. We all sin. However, sometimes we would like to believe our sin was unconscious when (if we are honest with ourselves and God) we knew that our actions or words would not be approved of by Him. We lie to ourselves, therefore making our sin a conscious choice. The world will see what we have done.

> *"So whatever you wish that others would do to you, do also to them, for this is the Law and the Prophets (Matthew 7:12).*

Knowledge of right and wrong is in our hearts and comes even more from the Holy Spirit which is given to us when we accept Christ. Pretending that we are unaware of the difference is an insult to the Father. We are saved by the grace of God through Christ's death on the cross. Our redemption is only the beginning. We are instructed to grow in the knowledge of our God and to draw closer in relationship to Him, therefore sinning less and showing His love more. We are set apart from the world for His work. We should be maturing as Christians knowing right from wrong, not staying in the same place.

As we mature, we become more aware when what we did or wanted to do was wrong. We become more aware of whom our Lord wants us to be as we stay in communication with Him and learn about Him. We do not remain babes in Christ constantly tripping and falling.

> *But solid food is for the mature, for those who have their powers of discernment trained by constant practice to distinguish good from evil (Hebrews 5:14).*

The Holy Spirit has been given to us to instruct and guide. Praying daily that the Holy Spirit will flow into and through us will ensure we know what is right and practice it with humility. None of us can get through this life without sinning, no matter how hard we try. Only God is perfect. Consciously or unconsciously, it is impossible for us to be perfectly sinless.

Praise God for His Grace. He looks at our hearts and knows our deepest thoughts. If we are honestly trying to grow closer to Him to do His work and to follow Christ's example, He will not hold unconscious or conscious sin against us.

As this world embraces evil and knowledge of right and wrong seems lost, we are the ones who become the moral compass to the world. We must know with certainty what is right (erring on the side of grace as God does) and we must show it to everyone.

We cannot afford for non-Christians (the world) to see us doing wrong. The time is already here when Christians are looked down upon and persecuted. The world will not turn from their wicked ways if we do not show them the difference that only Christ can make.

For the wages of sin is death, but the free gift of God is eternal life in Christ Jesus our Lord (Romans 6:23).

Forgiveness of Others

Pay attention to yourselves! If your brother sins, rebuke him, and if he repents, forgive him, and if he sins against you seven times in the day, and turns to you seven times, saying, 'I repent,' you must forgive him" (Luke 17:3-4).

Forgiveness is a difficult concept for us. We want to be forgiven by God and by others for our mistakes and sins. But how can we expect forgiveness and feel that we deserve forgiveness but, at the same time, have such a difficult time forgiving someone else?

When someone hurts us, be it a family member or someone

else, we experience a variety of emotions. We feel hurt, frustration, anger, and sometimes even thoughts of revenge. Family members may stop talking to each other. Grudges can be held for years, even though we know we are not following Christ's teaching or God's will.

God tells us that even if the offender does not repent or apologize, we still need to forgive. Christ on the cross forgave those who crucified Him. We can and should forgive those who hurt us no matter how difficult it might be. The Lord's Prayer does not just say "forgive us our trespasses." That sentence has a caveat when it goes on with "as we forgive those who trespass against us." If we only partially forgive will we be only partially forgiven? Something to think about.

And Jesus said, "Father, forgive them, for they know not what they do." And they cast lots to divide his garments (Luke 23:34).

It almost seems as if we enjoy being angry with those who hurt us. We wrap our hurt around us like a cloak and hold on for dear life. It protects us from future hurts. Anger justifies our actions. We don't want to forgive. We might even want to get back at the culprit and make them suffer the same pain that we have suffered.

If God were like us, He would have destroyed us long ago. Think of the horrible ways people have hurt God. Think of the sin that continues day after day in this world and yet, knowing in advance about this sin, God still sent His son to die on the cross so that we could be forgiven. When we confess our sins to Him, He forgives them, and He forgets that they even existed.

For if you forgive others their trespasses, your heavenly Father will also forgive you, but if you do not forgive others their trespasses, neither will your Father forgive your trespasses (Matthew 6:14-15).

How do we learn to forgive others the way God forgives us? Only by His grace and Holy Spirit are we able to put aside our hurt and anger. It may not be easy and it may take time, but there are things we can do to help ourselves become the forgiving people God wants us to be.

We must first make a conscious choice to forgive the person that hurt us. We must say it aloud, "I will forgive that person." Our old sinful self would say, "I will never forgive that person," but God wants us to change our thought patterns even before we are able to change our hearts. The more we say we won't forgive, the longer we will hurt and be angry. No good comes from holding a grudge.

Keep in mind that the alleged wrongdoer may not regret their actions or feel that they are in the wrong. They may not even know you are angry or may not know that you have forgiven them. It doesn't matter. For our own sakes, we need to forgive and believe that God will work on their hearts in the way He sees fit.

Saying that we will forgive doesn't mean we have. We are not there yet. We are only changing our thought processes to begin the healing and be open to Christ's teaching. If we can try to put ourselves in the other person's shoes, we may find a reason behind their actions and forgiveness can come more easily.

Bearing with one another and, if one has a complaint against another, forgiving each other; as the Lord has forgiven you, so you also must forgive (Colossians 3:13).

We are obligated to ask God to forgive the person who hurt us, and we can ask Him to take our hurt away. And here is the most difficult part; we must also ask God to bless the person who hurt us and to help us forgive them.

If we do this daily, God will honor our prayer, even our grudging prayer, and He will take our own hurt away. He will help us to forgive. Eventually the "I will forgive" becomes "I forgive." When we are finally able to truly forgive, our own hurt will be gone. We can use the space that the unforgiveness took up in our minds and hearts for better things for God.

Do not repay evil for evil or reviling for reviling, but on the contrary, bless, for to this you were called, that you may obtain a blessing (1 Peter 3:9).

Our lives are meant to be peaceful and abundant. There is no peace when there is no forgiveness. Blessings from God and abundant life don't come to us when we are hard and unforgiving.

Then Peter came up and said to him, "Lord, how often will my brother sin against me, and I forgive him? As many as seven times?" Jesus said to him, "I do not say to you seven times, but seventy times seven. "Therefore the kingdom of heaven may be compared to a king who wished to settle accounts with his servants. When he began to settle, one was brought to him who owed him ten thousand talents. And since he could not pay, his master ordered him to be sold, with his wife and children and all that he had, and payment to be made" (Matthew 18:21-25).

Forgiving the Ungrateful

But love your enemies, and do good, and lend, expecting nothing in return, and your reward will be great, and you will be sons of the Most High, for he is kind to the ungrateful and the evil (Luke 6:35).

If we will be honest with ourselves for a moment, we will find that when we give gifts or help someone out, we expect to be thanked. We want to be appreciated even if we say we don't care about that. Just a little appreciative acknowledgment makes us feel good. We do these kindnesses intending to forget about ever hearing from the receiver, but human nature kicks in. Suddenly, we find ourselves wondering why we were never thanked.

If we allow ourselves to become frustrated or angry at the recipient for the ingratitude, we know we are being illogical since we fully intended not to receive gratitude. However, we are human.

On the other hand, the recipient may have several reasons for not expressing gratitude to us. They may be embarrassed, uncomfortable, shy, or just busy. They may intend to thank us but don't get around to it, or they may believe that they did thank us.

Is it wrong to desire thanks?

Then Jesus answered, "Were not ten cleansed? Where are the nine? Was no one found to return and give praise to God except this foreigner?" And he said to him, "Rise and go your way; your faith has made you well" (Luke 17:17-19).

The problem is not that we want a little gratitude. The problem comes when not receiving positive acknowledgment for what we have done leads to disappointment, frustration or even anger.

Jesus expected those He helped to be grateful, and we should always show our gratitude to God and to others, but He didn't take His healing away from the ones who didn't return. Though we determine in our hearts to show our gratitude, we must be ready for the times when others do not.

When someone does not show gratitude, have they done us

harm? They didn't do us wrong since our kindness was done without expectation. If we are holding animosity against them for their lack of recognition, we need to ask for forgiveness for ourselves.

It is difficult enough to forgive people in our lives for past wrongs, supposed or real. Are we also expected to forgive those to whom we have done good and have neglected or forgotten to thank us? If we are disgruntled, treat them differently, or have unkind thoughts about them, it is time to turn our eyes to God and stop worrying about others.

Forgiving those we perceive to be ungrateful is a new subject for some of us. We may feel that our unhappiness with the ungrateful is righteous. After all, we did something good and got nothing in return. But we need to ask ourselves "wasn't that the point in the first place?"

But understand this, that in the last days there will come times of difficulty. For people will be lovers of self, lovers of money, proud, arrogant, abusive, disobedient to their parents, ungrateful, unholy (2 Timothy 3:1-2).

The general ungrateful attitude in the world today is only going to get worse. If people for which we do good are ungrateful to us, how much more ungrateful will they be for the grace and mercy of our Lord Jesus Christ?

Humankind is very self-focused and out for our own interests. This was prophesied and is obvious every day and everywhere. Christians must not emulate the world. We cannot become so focused on being thanked for what we do that we stop doing the good that God has asked of us. Our rewards all come from God.

For although they knew God, they did not honor him as God or give thanks to him, but they became futile in their thinking, and their foolish hearts were darkened (Romans 1:21).

The Lord's Prayer asks that God forgive us our trespasses as we forgive those who trespass against us. In addition to forgiving those who have wronged us, we can pray that God will forgive us for being ungrateful to Him as we forgive those who seem ungrateful to us. This may not seem like a big deal, but God is love and His forgiveness of our sins is what salvation is all about. We must love and forgive all perceived wrongs no matter how we feel or what has been done.

Betrayal

For if you forgive others their trespasses, your heavenly Father will also forgive you, but if you do not forgive others their trespasses, neither will your Father forgive your trespasses (Matthew 6:14-15).

Forgiving a betrayal is **more** than challenging. It can take herculean effort and is only truly accomplished with the help of the Holy Spirit. Realizing we have been betrayed is one of the worst experiences we will ever suffer. Betrayal makes us feel like we are breaking in two and will never recover. It hurts!

Most of us have felt betrayed at some point in our lives, and, with God's help, we can recover, but often the pain lingers long after we learn to forgive. Forgetting a betrayal is perhaps more difficult than forgiving.

Some betrayal is a momentary lapse, a falling into the devil's trap. Strange as it may seem, Judas Iscariot was not always a betrayer. God's word says that Satan entered him at that moment in time. If someone does us wrong, it may be a moment where evil has entered their thoughts and actions. Pray for them, forgive them, and love them. God will chase the evil out. Holding a grudge does no good for anyone.

> *Then Satan entered into Judas called Iscariot, who was of the number of the twelve. He went away and conferred with the chief priests and officers how he might betray him to them. And they were glad and agreed to give him money. So he consented and sought an opportunity to betray him to them in the absence of a crowd (Luke 22:3-6).*

Some betrayal is evil fighting against us. There is a force opposite of God in this world that we call Satan. God has told us about him and to be wary of his influence. He is a fallen angel who was thrown out of God's presence because of his pride. His pride continues to influence the world, making those who don't know God concerned only for their own pleasure and success. They think nothing of betraying someone for their own gain.

The closer we become to God, the more we are able to recognize the evil around us and seek God's protection. The Holy Spirit teaches us and makes us aware of those who are not trustworthy. We begin to feel in our 'gut' who is truthful and who is not, and we realize just who we are in a battle against. To survive and, more importantly, to **forgive betrayal, we need the armor of God and the power of the Holy Spirit.** We need a close relationship with our Lord to stand firm.

The most agonizing betrayal comes from those we trust. God asks us to forgive them as He has forgiven us and we say "How, God?" Forgiving a betrayal comes only through a lot of prayer and often much anguish. Forgiving a betrayal is almost as painful as the betrayal itself, **but true forgiveness through the Holy Spirit** gives us the ability to rejoice in the situation knowing that God makes good come out of difficulties for those who love Him. We may not see the good yet, but we know it is coming.

We are not required to be best buddies with the betrayer, but we are required to forgive them for our own wellbeing. Harboring hate in our hearts damages every part of our lives and relationships. It can affect future relationships, causing us to guard our hearts and feelings instead of choosing to trust. In the midst of betrayal, choose to trust God. He will take care of the betrayer and the betrayed.

Even my close friend in whom I trusted, who ate my bread, has lifted his heel against me (Psalm 41:9).

In our time on this earth, we will all feel betrayed at one time or another. Knowing this, we can be prepared, discerning the spirits of those around us and living a Godly life. We can treat others how we would like to be treated. God has laid it all out for us. Obey God and live. Betray others as Judas did and die. God will make it right for us in the end if we forgive.

A false witness will not go unpunished, and he who breathes out lies will not escape (Proverbs 19:5).

Chapter Eight

Lead Us Not into Temptation

Wrongful Thinking

And lead us not into temptation but deliver us from evil (Matthew 6:13)

This phrase in the Lord's Prayer is often said as if it were one thought or two ways of saying the same thing. But God does not lead us into temptation as we know from James 1:13 and being delivered from evil is a very different situation entirely. First look at temptation.

Let no one say when he is tempted, "I am being tempted by God," for God cannot be tempted with evil, and he himself tempts no one (James 1: 13).

If God does not lead us into temptation, why would Christ put that phrase into the prayer He taught the disciples? This may seem contradictory but looking at the Aramaic and Greek translations of this phrase makes it clearer to us. Here is a word study on the phrase by Chaim.

"Hence using the Dead Sea Scrolls rendering as a

guide we would find a more proper rendering of this phrase: Lead us not into temptation to be: Do not allow us to enter wrongful thinking or testing."[7]

We now understand that when we pray 'lead us not into temptation,' we are really asking God to protect us from making our own mistakes and to guide our minds into right thinking. We are asking Him to prevent us from using our free will to 'enter into' not only wrongful testing (being around what we know is bad for us) but also wrongful thinking. To know that God is protecting our minds is powerful and comforting.

Temptation and evil surround us constantly. According to **Merriam-Webster,** the word 'temptation,' as we use it now, is a *"strong urge or desire to have or do something, or something that causes a strong urge or desire to have or do something, especially something that is bad, wrong, or unwise."*

We often have this kind of temptation. We want food, drugs, money, fun, love, and so many other things. Giving in to temptation does not always lead to sin, but the problems begin when we are tempted to sin in order to get what we think we want. And so, we pray as Christ taught us, "lead us not into temptation but deliver us from evil," thinking that today's temptation is what was originally meant, but it is not.

We've looked at the subject of temptation; now, let's look at evil. God not only protects us from our own bad choices but also protects us from the evil that is in the world. Humanity today calls good evil and evil good. We are buffeted all around by people doing wrong but thinking it is right. We work with them, we live with them, we see them on television and movies, and we hear evil in our music. The world is evil, and we need to be delivered from it.

---

7 https://www.chaimbentorah.com/2015/12/word-study-lead-us-not-into-temptation-אנו-יסנ-לעת-אל/

Jesus, in His prayer, is encouraging us to pray for two different things. One is for protection from ourselves, and the other is for protection from the evil that comes from outside ourselves.

We can come before God and request these two protections, but we also have the responsibility to follow Christ's teaching to remove ourselves from places and things that tempt us. As much as is possible in living our daily lives, we must not give the devil any opportunity to confuse us, to scare us, to lie to us, or to draw us away from what is right.

Avoiding temptation makes life easier to resist evil when it presents itself. It is up to us to resist as we pray "lead us not into wrongful thinking or testing." Learning not to go along with the crowd can be challenging. Non-Christians will not understand why we choose not to get drunk or not to do drugs or sleep around. We will be judged and ridiculed. This is okay. This is persecution which Christ told us we would suffer. But the more we resist, the more the devil will flee. Christ is God the creator of Heaven and Earth. The devil is just a fallen angel. He is weak but with Christ we are strong.

> *Submit yourselves therefore to God. Resist the devil, and he will flee from you (James 4:7).*

There are ways we can stay strong in addition to avoiding places and things that tempt us. God's word tells us to arm ourselves for this battle as in Ephesians 6. This is a war for our very souls, but God has the armor.

> *Finally, be strong in the Lord and in the strength of his might. Put on the whole armor of God, that you may be able to stand against the schemes of the devil. For we do not wrestle against flesh and blood, but against the rulers, against the authorities, against the cosmic powers over this present darkness, against the*

> *spiritual forces of evil in the heavenly places. Therefore take up the whole armor of God, that you may be able to withstand in the evil day, and having done all, to stand firm. Stand therefore, having fastened on the belt of truth, and having put on the breastplate of righteousness, and, as shoes for your feet, having put on the readiness given by the gospel of peace. In all circumstances take up the shield of faith, with which you can extinguish all the flaming darts of the evil one; and take the helmet of salvation, and the sword of the Spirit, which is the word of God, praying at all times in the Spirit, with all prayer and supplication. To that end, keep alert with all perseverance, making supplication for all the saints (Ephesians 6:10-18).*

His word is our strength. God has our back, front, and all sides. We can stand firm, no matter what attacks us. We do that by being truthful, righteous, knowing the gospel, bringing peace wherever we are, having faith, relying on the Holy Spirit, and most of all, having God in our hearts and His forgiveness of our sins.

Repentance of our failures due to temptation means turning away permanently from the things we choose that made us fail and sin. It is a turning away from wrongful thinking and a turning toward God. We don't just stop sinning; we start living for God. We don't just stop hanging out with sinners; we start hanging out with those who believe as we do. We learn a different way to live and a different way to think. We need to change our wrongful thinking to God's thinking.

> *For because he himself has suffered when tempted, he is able to help those who are being tempted (Hebrews 2:18).*

It's All About Choices

"Enter by the narrow gate. For the gate is wide and the way is easy that leads to destruction, and those who enter by it are many" (Matthew 7:13).

Will we be among the many or the few? The choices we make determine the course of our future and will lead us to God or to death and destruction.

Our self-centered sinful nature will cause us to follow the wrong path, especially when we are young or immature. By the time we learn to reason, we can be so used to making selfish choices that we use our reasoning capabilities to justify our actions and they become right in our own eyes. It is not until we suffer the consequences of those choices that we realize they were not right, and they did not provide us with the joy and fun we thought they would.

Choices can save a life or ruin one. Every choice is a fork-in-the-road moment. Satan has made sin the easier choice. Our so-called friends who are choosing drugs and alcohol pressure us to join in. People doing wrong things often look like they are having fun and always encourage us to come along. That is the wide gate. Do not be fooled. Those choices are sin, and we are being tempted by Satan the enemy of God.

There is a way that seems right to a man, but its end is the way to death (Proverbs 14:12).

Ask anyone who has turned away from a life of wrong choices if the drama, the fear, the pain, the emotional upheaval, the lying, the jail time, the running, or the homelessness, was fun? The answer is no. Unfortunately choosing to get out of that life is much more difficult than getting in.

Alcoholics and addicts are taught to leave their old life behind. They do not hang out with their old friends or go to their old hangouts. They must separate themselves from that life to maintain their sobriety. It is a daily struggle that could have been avoided.

This is also a necessary choice for those who are committing crimes and/or sinning. The choice to leave behind all that we know and are comfortable with is one of the hardest choices to make, but it is the only way to truly change and find peace. We cannot have a foot in both the world of sin and the world of God.

"No one can serve two masters, for either he will hate the one and love the other, or he will be devoted to the one and despise the other. You cannot serve God and money (Matthew 6:24).

We cannot serve God and the world. The world may be our old friends, our old life, or our old loves. This is a difficult choice for those who have been raised as if wrong were right and Christianity was to be avoided. But as we mature, we come to understand that life is about choices.

No matter where we are in our lives today, we must evaluate where we should be and make choices to get there. For some, the choices will be easy. Maybe we will choose to be more faithful to church or read our Bible more so that we can grow closer to God and be who He wants us to be as Christians.

But for some of us, the choices can be more difficult. We may have to choose to separate ourselves from family members or those we love because they are addicts, dealers, thieves, or liars. We may have promised to stand by them and want to keep our promises, but God is telling us to allow Him to work in their lives. God is telling us to allow them to suffer the consequences of their choices or they will never choose Him. Only God can rescue the perishing.

The salvation of the righteous is from the LORD; he is their stronghold in the time of trouble (Psalm 37:39).

We must choose to remove one foot from either the sinful world or from God's path. Which will we choose when temptation comes our way?

Do not be deceived: God is not mocked, for whatever one sows, that will he also reap. For the one who sows to his own flesh will from the flesh reap corruption, but the one who sows to the Spirit will from the Spirit reap eternal life (Galatians 6:7-8).

Tempted to Worry

"Therefore I tell you, do not be anxious about your life, what you will eat or what you will drink, nor about your body, what you will put on. Is not life more than food, and the body more than clothing? Look at the birds of the air: they neither sow nor reap nor gather into barns, and yet your heavenly Father feeds them. Are you not of more value than they?" (Matthew 6:25-26).

The tendency to worry is a temptation. It separates us from God and is one of those tools used by our adversary the devil to destroy our faith and draw us away from God, which is exactly what temptation or being drawn into wrong thinking (worry) does. Worry is the worst of wrong thinking for the Christian. The opposite of worry is faith.

There are more than 300 verses in the Bible encouraging us not to worry, which, according to Strong's concordance, means to be divided or distracted, to be troubled with, or to care for.

Overall, everyone in this world, even Christians, spend approximately five years of a 64-year lifespan worrying.[8] It

---
8 https://www.iol.co.za/entertainment/celebrity-news/how-much-time-do-you-spend-worrying-1904679

is understandable that non-Christians would worry since they don't believe in a loving Father who is watching out for them and helping them in their difficulties. But we should be different.

God does not want our attention to be divided between Him and the things of this world or to be troubled by things out of our control. When we worry about something, He wants us to bring it to Him. Letting go of our worries to God can strengthen our faith when we watch for the blessings that come.

Distraction is something that, though a natural human behavior, is a trick of the devil to separate us from God. Dividing our attention between worldly needs and God's care for us makes us anxious and troubled. We cannot live an abundant life while our attentions are divided and our hearts are full of fear.

God does not say that if we worry, we will not receive the Kingdom. Worry, when given to God, can bring us closer to Him as He encourages us to trust and not to waste our time in worry. It is not a sign of lack of faith but an arrow pointing us to ask for more faith. However, the temptation to worry without putting our faith in God can lead down a dangerous path.

> *And which of you by being anxious can add a single hour to his span of life? (Matthew 6:27).*

We don't usually think of worry as a temptation, but clearly when things are not going as we would like them to, try as we might not to worry, we are often tempted beyond control to take our minds off God's care and become distracted by worry and stress. Don't forget the true definition of temptation. ***Do not allow us to enter wrongful thinking or testing."***

The prince of darkness wants to harm our relationship with God. He wants to steal our joy. He wants us to enter into wrong thinking and testing and then accuses us of a lack of faith so that we feel even worse in the end.

The devil will take every opportunity we give him to make us miserable. He will try to turn us from God, but if that is not possible and we stand firm, he will try to divert our focus away from God and steal our joy by making us anxious about our problems.

Viewing times of worry as temptation and not as a human weakness can help us fight against it. Faith is a fruit of the Holy Spirit, and the original Greek word used for faith means something that must be asked for. We can ask for more faith from the Holy Spirit while we resist the devil's temptation to worry about those things over which we have no control.

Do not be anxious about anything, but in everything by prayer and supplication with thanksgiving let your requests be made known to God (Philippians 4:6).

Obedience

God's Word tells us how sin entered the world and that we must repent of our sin to be forgiven and live in a right relationship with Him. It tells us how Christ died for our sins and that we must accept Him into our hearts and lives. To repent means to turn away from the sins of our past and our continued sins with which we struggle.

God sent His Son, Jesus Christ to teach us how to live a holy life free from sin and pleasing to God. He will forgive new sins each time we repent but turning from sin is not enough. We must choose to leave sin behind and turn **toward** God. We cannot continue sinning and asking for forgiveness, never truly intending to stop the sin. It's all about what is in our hearts. God is not fooled.

"If you love me, you will keep my commandments" (John 14:15).

Complete obedience to the word of God has always been a struggle, these days in particular because many of the sins we are tempted with are deemed acceptable by the world. We tell ourselves that "everyone does it," therefore, it can't really be a sin.

We have created a list of sins where one is worse than others based on what we see, read, and hear. "I'm not a murderer so surely I am ok." These statements are lies of the devil. He knows that we are easily led by what the crowds around us are doing even when the actions are evil in God's sight.

We must stand on God's word, not on what the world has decided is admissible. The world changes, but God does not change. Our eternity is not graded on a curve. It is not a grading system whereby we might get a **C** but still make it to heaven. Every sin is repulsive to God. He will not accept those who commit them, the end! Accepting Christ and turning **from** sin and turning **to** God is the only way to salvation. Those who turn away from sin but do not turn to God are still sinners.

> *"Not everyone who says to me, 'Lord, Lord,' will enter the kingdom of heaven, but the one who does the will of my Father who is in heaven" (Matthew 7:21).*

Trying to justify our sin is lying to God. In church we learn about repentance, forgiveness, and obedience. Walking out of church and continuing to sin is a serious problem. If we occasionally give in to temptation while sincerely trying not to sin, He will forgive us, but God knows the truth in our hearts. He cannot be deceived, and so we pray for Him to help us avoid wrong thinking.

> *For all that is in the world — <u>the desires of the flesh and the desires of the eyes and pride of life</u> — is not from the Father but is from the world (1 John 2:16).*

There is a multitude of sins listed in the Bible, and they fall into three categories. The first is **desires of the flesh** or fleshly desires like sexual immorality (sex before marriage), adultery, sensuality, orgies, homosexuality, drunkenness, and lack of self-control. These are things our flesh desires and that we think will make us feel good.

Then there are the **desires of our eyes,** the things we see, want, and take. Some of these sins would include theft, coveting, idolatry, sorcery, jealousy, rivalries, envy, love of money, and greed. We are a very greedy people in some parts of the world.

Last, there is the **pride of life**. Pride that causes us to see ourselves as more important than others is not of God. Some of these sins are arrogance, being abusive, heartless, reckless, swollen with conceit, appearing to be Godly but not Godly.

All sins are equal in God's sight, and He has reasons that they are sin. We may not understand His reason, but we can be assured it is for our good. There is no degree of human badness with God. Lying is the same as murder. Sex before marriage is the same as stealing. Sin is sin. We must trust that God's will is what is best for us. Though we are all tempted at times, God will help us resist temptation. Look at 1 Corinthians again.

> *No temptation has overtaken you that is not common to man. God is faithful, and he will not let you be tempted beyond your ability, but with the temptation he will also provide the way of escape, that you may be able to endure it (1 Cor. 10:13).*

God is not mean-spirited, calling these actions and feelings 'sin' to ruin our fun. God wants us to be healthy and happy, living productive lives and bringing others into the Kingdom. He gave us His Son as an example, and we have His Holy Spirit to mentor us. We should continually ask for forgiveness and for strength to withstand the tricks and lies of the devil.

If we say we have no sin, we deceive ourselves, and the truth is not in us. If we confess our sins, he is faithful and just to forgive us our sins and to cleanse us from all unrighteousness. If we say we have not sinned, we make him a liar, and his word is not in us (1 John 1:8-10).

With God in our hearts, we know right from wrong. It is our responsibility to be honest and choose to do the right thing instead of what we think might temporarily give us pleasure. We pray "Lord do not allow us to enter into wrongful thinking."

So whoever knows the right thing to do and fails to do it, for him it is sin (James 4:17).

We Can Overcome

Corinthians tells us that these temptations (wrong thinking) are common to everyone and that God knows what is tempting us. He will not allow us to be tempted beyond what we can withstand, although it often seems so. There is always another choice available to us that will be pleasing to God. God makes a way of escape for every temptation.

Wrong thinking and testing come to each of us daily. We may not recognize them as they sneak up on us looking like something good. Temptations are directly connected to the decisions we make. If we choose to yield when tempted, they will eventually cause us to sin or do harm to ourselves or others.

The temptations to sin that may affect us range from what some may call a white lie, to an alcoholic having a drink, to the desire to take a life. We are tempted to do and say things that we think will get us **out** of trouble or make our lives easier when, in reality, they get us into more trouble and make our lives more difficult. We are tempted to say and do things that we think will bring us happiness and fun but bring us pain and despair. Drugs, sex, and alcohol are strong temptations in the world we live in today and are not even considered sin in some circles. But they are sin. God has made known to us exactly what sin is and what sin is not.

We are weak in mind and body and the devil uses the world's views of right and wrong to convince us that we are not really sinning or that giving in to a momentary temptation is no big deal. But Christ in us is strong as we pray 'lead us not into temptation.' Convincing ourselves that we are doing nothing wrong is lying to ourselves and is mocking God.

We know right from wrong. We know that just because the world says something is acceptable doesn't mean that it is acceptable to God. Why do we play this game? Why do we allow the devil to tempt us and convince us to do what we know is wrong?

Watch and pray that you may not enter into temptation. The spirit indeed is willing, but the flesh is weak" (Matthew 26:41).

When we call on God to show us the way out of temptation, we will feel in our hearts and souls when something is not right. He will tell us by our consciences, by our knowledge, and by His word what is right and what is wrong. The choice to bring the temptation to God is our choice to make. Do not be deceived. God is not tempting us. Temptation is from the deceiver, the accuser, and the liar.

In our lives we make choices. We can choose to go to places that will bring us to temptation. We can choose to be with people who will tempt us or whose behavior will tempt us. We can choose to avoid talking temptation over with God. We can fool ourselves into believing that little lies don't matter, but the truth is that there is no hierarchy of sin in the eyes of God. All sin is equal.

We have free will to do these things and we are tempted and pressured on all sides to do them. Evil whispers in our ears, 'It's ok. Everyone is doing it. Just this once won't hurt." Do not listen to anything that goes against Christ's teaching. Read the word of God so you will know how He wants you to walk.

And give no opportunity to the devil (Ephesians 4:27).

What can we do then? We must pray and strengthen our relationship with the Father. We must be honest with ourselves, and we must stay away from people and places that will tempt us. We always have a choice. We always have a way of escape given to us by God. We can overcome.

Little children, you are from God and have overcome them, for he who is in you is greater than he who is in the world (1 John 4:4).

Chapter Nine

But Deliver Us from Evil

But Really, What Is Evil?

Woe to those who call evil good and good evil, who put darkness for light and light for darkness, who put bitter for sweet and sweet for bitter! (Isaiah 5:20).

Isaiah is describing our world today so clearly. The world does not seem to understand the meaning of the word 'evil.' There are many Greek words used in the Bible for 'evil' but 'Poneo' is the most prominent and has several definitions attached to it. From the New American Standard Exhaustive Concordance, we find the following:

Word Origin: from poneó (to toil)
Definition: toilsome, bad
Translation: bad, crimes, envious, envy, evil, evil one, evil things, malignant, more evil, more wicked, vicious, wicked, wicked man, wicked thing, worthless.

People calling evil good and good evil have been around a long time, but just watch the news for a couple of days and see how this blindness has progressed. People avoid even using the word 'evil' because it is no longer politically correct.

If we look at some of the translations of 'evil' in the Bible, we find it can even stand for what some consider not sin at all such as envy or things that are worthless or toilsome (tiresome). God knows what evil is, but do we?

Isaiah said woe to those who reverse good and evil. We say woe to our world today. The world considers to be our prerogative and, at times, even our responsibility, things like worthless pursuits, wicked actions or thoughts, vicious words, and things that are crimes against God and man. We must not close our eyes to the evil around us.

When did the word 'evil' become taboo? This did not come from God. Humanity works very hard to ignore God's teachings and our consciences so that we can feel good about ourselves. Obviously, the word *evil* ascribed to our activities or thinking does not make us feel good about ourselves so we do away with it. If we don't call it evil, then it must be ok.

The fear (respect) of the Lord is hatred of evil. Pride and arrogance and the way of evil and perverted speech I hate (Proverbs 8:13).

Since God hates evil, we who respect Him and love Him are to hate evil, too. He hates worthless pursuits and vicious words just as much as crimes such as murder. Remember there is no hierarchy of sin with God. Sin is sin. Evil is evil. God does not accept and will not tolerate such behavior from His children.

We fool ourselves when we think looking at dirty photos online is not a big deal. We fool ourselves when we seek instant money by playing the lottery or telling a 'white' lie. We fool ourselves when we are envious of our neighbor's lifestyle and think we deserve more. But God is not fooled. He is not pleased. He does not say to Himself, "Well, that's not so bad."

> *Do not be deceived: God is not mocked, for whatever one sows, that will he also reap. For the one who sows to his own flesh will from the flesh reap corruption, but the one who sows to the Spirit will from the Spirit reap eternal life (Galatians 6:7-8).*

As Christians in this generation, we face new evils that were not even considered in the past. Technology, although it brings a lot of good, also brings a lot of evil and opportunities for evil. Never before have we been able to see and hear everything that is going on in our world or in the government instantaneously. Never before have people doing evil deeds been able to promote their actions and deceive us into thinking they are right.

Because this information bombards us so rapidly and continuously we don't have time to pray or study God's word before either jumping into the fray or not. No wonder God wants us to be still and know that He is God. He knew this was coming. He knew we needed time to think about His point of view of what is happening on earth today. We must be constantly in His word so we are ready to ward off evil. God will deliver us if we are ready.

When we take the time to draw closer to God and to follow His teachings, He will deliver us from evil. He will make us aware of what type of evil is being set before us. He will help us discern what is good and right and just. We need to ask Him for discernment and knowledge and the wisdom to know what to do with them.

> *Abstain from every form of evil (1 Thessalonians 5:22).*

It is not rocket science (another important technology). We need to recognize evil and call it what it is. We need to leave it behind us while we strive to do the next right thing every minute of every day.

In the days before the flood, God was grieved with man. Now we must show Him that His children, who are called by His name, know what evil is and we will stand against it.

> *The Lord saw that the wickedness of man was great in the earth, and that every intention of the thoughts of his heart was only evil continually. And the Lord was sorry that he had made man on the earth, and it grieved him to his heart (Genesis 5:6).*

Darkness in the World

It is difficult to understand that this world created by a good God is under the control or the power of Satan. God indeed created all things and placed in the Garden of Eden His creations the first man and the first woman. Once they brought sin into the world, evil became the norm. They gave up their relationship with God and followed after their own choosing.

The world came under the power of darkness, and its evil remains today. Satan, as the beautiful, yet prideful and evil angel, was cast out of heaven to earth and now rules over humankind until Christ's return. He does not rule over those of us who have renewed our relationship with God by asking Christ into our hearts.

Our many problems, whether financial, physical, or mental, all come because evil entered this world and took temporary control of humankind. The temptation to lie, cheat, and steal, and all sins, come from the power of darkness. We call him Satan, but whatever we call him (it), he wants us to lose out on the gift of eternal life with Christ. He is the enemy of God.

> *You adulterous people! Do you not know that*

friendship with the world is enmity with God? Therefore whoever wishes to be a friend of the world makes himself an enemy of God (James 4:4).

God's word tells us that we, His followers, are not to be of this world. We are not to be worldly in our desires and our lifestyles. We are not to live like those who do **not** follow Christ. We are not to be influenced by the powers of darkness.

We are surrounded by evil. If we wonder why life is difficult, evil is the reason. The power that is over this world is trying to draw us away from God. Everywhere we turn evil will be there. It is impossible to be with Christians all the time, and even then, evil can creep in. We are all sinners. We are not perfect. Though forgiven, we still find ourselves doing what we know is wrong in the eyes of God. It is no wonder our Lord Jesus added the words 'deliver us from evil' in His prayer.

I have said these things to you, that in me you may have peace. In the world you will have tribulation. But take heart; I have overcome the world" (John 16:33).

We have the good news of Jesus Christ. His death on the cross for our sins saves us from continuing to live evil lives. We are covered by His blood. If we follow Him, we are safe in our salvation and we can enjoy His blessings. We still must deal with the evil world around us. We will have tribulation, but we can also have peace.

Evil tells us the "world is changing, getting better, and people are more accepting of each other." Their words tickle our ears. The changes and our acceptance are so gradual we don't even notice that Christian views of sin are wavering. The unthinkable becomes acceptable and finally celebrated. We are becoming complacent when we encounter sin. We have been convinced sin is not sin anymore. Staying separate from the world and relying wholly on God's Holy Spirit to guide us is our hope of deliverance.

We know that we are from God, and the whole world lies in the power of the evil one (1 John 5:19).

The lives of evildoers may seem exciting and enticing. That is one of the many tricks of Satan and one of the many lies used to draw us away from the truth. Sin often masquerades as good or fun. It often seems harmless. Do not be fooled by these lies.

God is not mean. He does not want our lives to be drudgery. He knows what will harm us and what will help us in our lives. He knows what will bring us true joy. We are all different, and yet sin is the same for each of us and will hurt us in the long run. This does not mean that we all act the same, do the same things, or say things in the same way. We are to be ourselves as God made us, striving to follow Christ, and staying away from sin.

Again Jesus spoke to them, saying, "I am the light of the world. Whoever follows me will not walk in darkness, but will have the light of life" (John 8:12).

Darkness—not the darkness when the sun goes down—but the darkness of evil is where we will live if we continue to sin. The light is where all good things happen, and Christ is the light. We must leave the darkness, repent of our sins, and move into the light where we can see the truth and not go groping in the darkness.

Evil continues to spread. Until Christ returns, the world will not get better. Sins are becoming acceptable. Children choose their own gender. Movies win awards showing men and women doing evil things. Cults and the occult are rampant. Our schools teach other religions and evolution but not Christianity. Men are with men and women are with women, and babies are killed daily.

It is time for a revival of the world's love for Christ. The Good News must be told and shown wherever we can. We must worship in spirit and in truth. And we must pray for deliverance from the evil one who is working through humankind. God does ultimately win. He will take control once again. Will we be with Him?

The times of ignorance God overlooked, but now he commands all people everywhere to repent (Acts 17:30).

Blaming God

And we are writing these things so that our joy may be complete. This is the message we have heard from him and proclaim to you, that God is light, and in him is no darkness at all (1 John 1:4-5).

God is love and light. He delivered us out of darkness and gave us eternal life with Him when we accepted the sacrifice of His son Jesus Christ. All good gifts come from God. He loves us. We are His children, His creation, and He gives us hope and the security of knowing that He is always with us. We are followers of Christ, and yet evil abounds. These statements may seem like platitudes, but they are truth. God is love and light. Christians have this light. The world is in darkness.

God gave individuals free will even to make bad choices or to hang around with unsavory people. We know that death, disease, poverty, starvation, etc. are a part of this world. But there is no darkness in God. Darkness is in the enemy of God. We are at war with the darkness.

But some think that God is taking away our happiness, that

He takes away our jobs, our family, etc. We often hear phrases referring to God giving and taking away. It is disturbing to hear this misuse of scripture. God is not to blame for wars and starving children. We need to be well-versed on this subject if we want to counter the arguments of unbelievers who question the bad that happens in our world.

> *The LORD kills and brings to life; he brings down to Sheol and raises up. The LORD makes poor and makes rich; he brings low and he exalts (1 Samuel 2:6-7).*

The notion that God takes away or brings low can be disheartening taken out of context. To think that a loving Father would arbitrarily decide to take something away from us and make us miserable does not make sense. And it is not true. God is love and light. In Him there is no darkness at all.

When this idea comes up in God's word, it is brought by a person like Hannah in 1 Samuel above, who is praying, or Job when things are not going well for him. In both cases, they are recognizing God's mighty power over everything and giving Him glory because He is all-powerful. They are not accusing Him of being unkind.

He does have power over what is given and what is taken away. However, God Himself does not take good gifts away from His children. He gives them. He delivers us from evil.

In this world, God will allow negative things to happen so that ultimately, we will live a more abundant life and have a closer relationship with Him. Allowing the evil of the world to move around us and to affect our lives is a very different concept than snatching away something good just to make us miserable or teach us a lesson. That is not God's nature.

We know in Job's case that the devil was the one doing the taking (allowed by God). Even though Job said it was the Lord who had taken away his blessings, what was implied is that the Lord had and has the power to allow or disallow blessings to be taken.

And he said, "Naked I came from my mother's womb, and naked shall I return. The LORD gave, and the LORD has taken away; blessed be the name of the LORD" (Job 1:21).

We must be aware of the difference in meaning as we serve God and learn to trust Him. If we were to believe that at any given moment God would decide to take a blessing away, trusting Him would be impossible. But God does not take His blessings away. He allows things to change as the natural world causes (laws of nature) and as we make bad choices in our daily lives.

In the natural world, if we are hit by a falling brick, we are going to suffer pain and perhaps death. God is not taking away our life, but He is not waving a magic wand to stop the brick from falling, either.

We must stop blaming God for taking things away or causing bad things to happen. Remember where we live and who is the ruler of this world. Evil took charge when humanity fell from grace. We serve an all-powerful God. He is not weak or mushy. He could do anything He wanted but He chose to send His son to die for our sins, for our mistakes, for our faults and crimes. He chose to bring us back into His loving arms, and He is working on every person in all the world all the time to bring them back, too.

God is holy and just. We pray for and await the day when He will rule and reign here on earth. In the meantime, we pray that He will deliver us from evil and help us to make good choices to stay away from the temptations of this world that can cause negative things to happen.

In addition, we are God's hands and feet here on earth. We can stop some of the negative forces at work and do good to help bring about His blessings. God sends us to stop the evil.

We must be the ones to do the good work and spread the good news.

Praise and thank God for His blessings and put the blame for taking things away and making life difficult where it belongs. God gives good gifts to His children.

> *If you then, who are evil, know how to give good gifts to your children, how much more will your Father who is in heaven give good things to those who ask him! (Matthew 7:11).*

Out of the Blue

> *Trust in the LORD with all your heart, and do not lean on your own understanding. In all your ways acknowledge him, and he will make straight your paths (Proverbs 3:5-6).*

There are curveballs in life that come at us out of the blue. "Didn't see that coming" is a phrase we hear today when we are surprised by some unforeseen event. Some of these are good surprises, but sometimes we suffer setbacks and pain from evil that we were unprepared for, and in those times, we must hold onto our faith in God more strongly than ever. Satan is trying to destroy our relationship with the Father.

'**But deliver us from evil**' is the second half of a sentence which begins with '**Lead us not into temptation**' in the Lord's Prayer. Though the two parts seem similar, the last part is a very different request of God.

When life is going along smoothly but suddenly our rental house is put up for sale or we have a great boss who quits and is replaced with a sociopath, our world can go spinning off to a dark place of worry and fear. We may be driving along and suddenly hit a boy on a skateboard who is texting unaware.

These are unexpected evils that can shake our faith and knock us back on our heels. These are the times we cry out "Why God? We were doing so well."

Blessed is the man who remains steadfast under trial, for when he has stood the test he will receive the crown of life, which God has promised to those who love him (James 1:12).

Instead of falling backward, we need to fall on our knees before God and ask Him to deliver us from these trials. The Lord's Prayer does not say that evil will not come to us. In the prayer, we are asking for deliverance from the evil and the trials that happen to everyone. God does not bring evil to us and He does not tempt us or try to cause us to fail. We know the devil is at work in these situations to cause us to lose our faith. We must build up our armor of God by prayer and thanksgiving. He will deliver us through evil times.

When the righteous cry for help, the Lord hears and delivers them out of all their troubles (Psalm 34:17).

Then they cried to the Lord in their trouble, and he delivered them from their distress (Psalm 107:6).

Our trust that God will bring about good from these instances must remain steadfast. Hope is one of the greatest benefits of knowing Him and is a fruit provided by the Holy Spirit. We have hope that the world does not have. Lean on God. When trials come out of the blue, it may seem as though He is nowhere to be found, but He has not abandoned us.

Remember that the word 'hope' in the Bible translates as a certainty. This is not the uncertain hope we have today. We can be certain that God is working in our lives.

The funny thing about trials, temptations, or any bad

thing that happens suddenly is that good circumstances and good gifts can come just as suddenly. We don't know what tomorrow holds, whether good or bad, but we do know that God has gotten us through trials before and He will again. Trust God. He will deliver us! Look for the ways that He is working it all out for our good.

Most of us can look back at the bad times in our lives and see the good that followed. Hope, faith, and trust in God during the surprises that knocked us down helps us get up and remain strong. It only takes a moment for things to turn around and become good instead of bad. Never give up.

> *And we know that for those who love God all things work together for good, for those who are called according to his purpose (Romans 8:28).*

Bad things will happen. They can come as an 'out of the blue' phone call or visit, an accident, an illness, or death. But God is still the Lord, and He is working in this evil world to bring about His purpose through us and through others.

We love the Lord and we are called according to His purpose. His purpose is for all to come to know Him as their Lord and Savior. The trials and the evil that Satan uses to draw us away will instead be used by God to draw us closer. Our faith during these times and the good that comes from it will reveal to others the glory of God.

> *For I consider that the sufferings of this present time are not worth comparing with the glory that is to be revealed to us (Romans 8:18).*

Do good and pray that He will deliver us from evil and that He will strengthen us when evil comes. We will have bad things happen sometimes out of the blue, but God will deliver us! Praise be to God.

A Thief and a Liar

But I am afraid that as the serpent deceived Eve by his cunning, your thoughts will be led astray from a sincere and pure devotion to Christ (2 Corinthians 11:3).

Some Christians believe that the deceiver of this world has no influence on those who believe in Christ. We do know that Satan deceives the world and those who don't believe in God. Unbelievers are influenced and drawn away from God and are deceived and blinded to the truth about Christ.

But Christians are also attacked by Satan as he tries to steal our very souls back from the salvation provided by Christ's death on the cross for our sins. We must be aware of Satan's deceit and pray to be delivered from his influence.

We see that even though Adam and Eve had a perfect relationship with God, they also had free will and were deceived into breaking their covenant with Him. If God's first humans living in a perfect setting could be tempted to disobey, we, living in this sinful world, most certainly can and are tempted daily.

When he (Satan) lies, he speaks out of his own character, for he is a liar and the father of lies (John 8:44b).

Satan is evil incarnate in as much as he influences those around us. He has no truth in him, and he seeks to destroy those who follow Christ. To our detriment, there is not a lot of teaching or preaching about the devil these days. But the warnings to us are throughout God's word. Christ cautioned us and informed us of Satan's intent. The disciples and the apostle Paul spoke of his rebellion against God and told us to be wary. Yet, we don't want to talk about the devil for fear of offending the hearer. That is truly one of the most successful tricks of the evil one.

Some people believe in God, but not the devil. This is not scriptural and is another one of Satan's biggest deceptions. If there is no devil, then there is no hell so we can go on doing as we please, living lives of sin.

Some feel that talking about Satan or hell is a scare tactic and will drive people away from Christ instead of towards Him. They believe that we should only talk about Christ's great love. This is also a great lie designed to weaken our knowledge and faith. Making us fearful of talking about Satan allows him to draw people into his darkness because they are not knowledgeable enough to be wary or to pray against him. The less we know about him, the less we can fight.

> ***The thief comes only to steal and kill and destroy. I came that they may have life and have it abundantly (John 10:10).***

Christ came to destroy the devil's work, the devil's deception of Adam and Eve, and his power over us. He came to give us the life we were intended to have when we were created. If we take Satan out of the equation, there is no reason for Christ to have died. We cannot allow our eyes to be blinded to the fact that the devil is the cause of all evil, pain, and suffering. How can we fight an enemy we know nothing about? Information is power.

Even sports teams study their opponents before a game. We must know the tricks, the lies, and the ways he will try to steal from us and be ready. We cannot give him any opportunity to affect our lives or our witness for Christ. We must be bolder in telling the world to beware. This is one of the reasons the world is as it is. We are told to preach the gospel, and this is part of it.

Satan is here to steal the souls of the world and of Christians too, but if he can't steal our souls, he will settle for stealing our joy. We may think we are protected, and it is true that the Holy Spirit strengthens us to resist, but we also live in this evil world and are affected by what is happening around us. Even though we have accepted Christ into our hearts and lives and been forgiven of our sins, we still can choose which way we will turn in every situation. Remember, every choice is a fork in the road between good and evil.

And give no opportunity to the devil (Ephesians 4:27).

God is love, and telling of His love is the ultimate message, but we can't avoid learning about and being ready to fight against His enemy. God's enemy is our enemy and he will use every trick and every lie and will try to steal every joy from believers to cause us to join him in hell. Yes, hell exists and is totally separate from God and His glory, and those who turn from God will spend eternity there in more misery and pain than was ever felt here on earth.

Satan is a thief and a liar. Be aware, be watchful, and be prayerful. When we are depressed, angry, fearful, mean, or any other way that is opposite of God's love, we are falling for Satan's tricks and allowing his influence into our lives. He may be the god of this world, but he is not our God, and he is not even a god at all. He is only a fallen sinful angel whose pride caused him to lose everything. At the final judgment, he will be cast into the pit forever.

Be sober-minded; be watchful. Your adversary the devil prowls around like a roaring lion, seeking someone to devour (1 Peter 5:8).

Chapter Ten

For Thine is the Kingdom and the Power and Glory Forever

Our View of God

For his invisible attributes, namely, his eternal power and divine nature, have been clearly perceived, ever since the creation of the world, in the things that have been made. So they (we) are without excuse (Romans 1:20 Jenni's version).

Most Christians view God as a loving father. He loves us beyond our comprehension. He sent His only son to die to bring us back into fellowship with Him. He cares for every aspect of our lives, leads and guides us, and gives us eternal life with Him. He gives us peace and comfort.

We can speak in intimate terms with God and can call Him our Father as Christ did. We can have a personal relationship with Him, even though He is a spiritual being and not physically present. But this closeness can sometimes limit our view of His true greatness and power.

As Christians living in a world where things are seen, felt, and known, spiritual truths are difficult to understand. We tend to think of God more in human terms than the omnipotent (almighty, all-powerful, invincible) spiritual being that He is. When we limit God as we are limited, we lose faith in Him, and the deceiver can bring worry and stress to our minds. But God has all power and glory in His Kingdom.

> *Thus says the LORD, your Redeemer, who formed you from the womb: "I am the LORD, who made all things, who alone stretched out the heavens, who spread out the earth by myself" (Isaiah 44:24).*

God is the Lord and the King over all the universe that He created. We must not make Him small in our minds but must have reverence for His spiritual enormity. When we worship Him, it should show how much we understand the incredibleness of what has been done for us.

Since God is a spiritual being and we are created in His image, we are also spirit. It is our spirit that lives on with Him after our bodies die and it is our spirit that communes with Him now. It is our spirit that feels His presence as we worship Him.

Knowing who God really is and who we are in Him can build our faith and create a stronger personal relationship with the loving God we already know. We may live in a world where walls hold us back, but our spirits don't have walls and when we truly know God, all things are possible.

> *Where shall I go from your Spirit? Or where shall I flee from your presence? (Psalm 139:7).*

The God of power and glory has plans that are bigger than just what He can do for us. Thinking of God as omnipotent (almighty, all-powerful, invincible) and omnipresent (present everywhere at the same time) reminds us that our lives are in the great hands of the Almighty God.

And what is the immeasurable greatness of his power toward us who believe, according to the working of his great might (Ephesians 1:19).

God has promised to guide, protect, and help us by His Holy Spirit in this world. He has promised that we will live eternally with Him if we love and follow Him. His son took our penalty upon His own body so that we can call our indescribable creator 'Father' and experience a relationship that is close and loving. But He is so much more.

All things were made through him, and without him was not anything made that was made (John 1:3).

Though there is great evil in the world, it will not overtake us. We have the powerful and glorious God as our Father, Lord, and King. He is not weak. He is not human. He is not small.

"I am the Alpha and the Omega," says the Lord God, "who is and who was and who is to come, the Almighty" (Revelation 1:8).

The Importance of Praise

Praise the LORD! Praise God in his sanctuary; praise him in his mighty heavens! Praise him for his mighty deeds; praise him according to his excellent greatness! Praise him with trumpet sound; praise him with lute and harp! Praise him with tambourine and dance; praise him with strings and pipe! Praise him with sounding cymbals; praise him with loud clashing

> *cymbals! Let everything that has breath praise the Lord! Praise the Lord! (Psalm 150:1-6).*

This section of the Lord's prayer is a call to praise and worship our Father. Human praise is something we crave in our own lives and something we give out to others when they have done things we consider praiseworthy. It is such a normal everyday activity and desire that we rarely wonder why it is important to us.

When we praise God, it is altogether different. God desires our praise, and His word says He inhabits our praise. We were created in the image of God, so receiving praise must be something important also to have been so ingrained in us. It must be part of God's nature. We could have been created without the need to praise or the need to receive praise. Why did God place that craving in us?

It would be an interesting world if we didn't need to receive or give praise to each other. Would we be driven to do good or to work at our jobs if we didn't receive praise of some kind? To us, praise is thankfulness, recognition, and something that makes us feel good. It is a motivator to us for sure, but God does not need motivation. So why is praising God important to Him?

> *Oh come, let us sing to the LORD; let us make a joyful noise to the rock of our salvation! Let us come into his presence with thanksgiving; let us make a joyful noise to him with songs of praise! For the LORD is a great God, and a great King above all gods. In his hand are the depths of the earth; the heights of the mountains are his also. The sea is his, for he made it, and his hands formed the dry land (Psalm 95:1-5).*

Praise to God involves thankfulness for His mercy and greatness. It is recognizing what God has done for us and praising Him just for whom He is (even if He never did anything for us). The importance of praising God is that it takes our minds off our own negative thoughts. We spend a great deal of time thinking about our own problems, asking for God's help, worrying and fretting. Praising God turns those thoughts outward and upward. Giving Him glory reminds us of just how much He has done in our lives for our good.

Praising others reminds us that they have value and to praise God shows Him that we highly value Him above all else. If we neglect to praise Him, what does that say about what we value? Where is our treasure stored?

"Through him then let us continually offer up a sacrifice of praise to God, that is, the fruit of lips that acknowledge his name" (Hebrews 13:15).

Praise requires sacrifice from us. It is a sacrifice of time, effort and thought. To praise God is to focus our minds and hearts on Him and to acknowledge His sovereignty. It shows that we know He is not just a friend and helper. His kindness, grace, and mercy to us do not diminish our recognition of His strength, power, and authority over all.

Who is this King of glory? The Lord, *strong and mighty, the* Lord, *mighty in battle! Lift up your heads, O gates! And lift them up, O ancient doors, that the King of glory may come in. Who is this King of glory? The* Lord *of hosts, he is the King of glory! Selah (Psalm 24:8-10).*

When we praise God in song or in worship, in thanksgiving, with instruments, or in prayer we are inviting His presence to be with us. God is spirit, and His spirit joins in and inhabits our praise. Acknowledging that His is the Kingdom, power and glory brings Him joy and opens us up to a greater Holy

Spirit influence in our lives.

We cannot be silent in our worship in the face of such a great Creator. We cannot ignore His majesty, His mercies or His love. All that we are and all that we have come from God. Our hope for the future and for eternity is in Him. He desires our praise, and He *deserves* our praise. He created us with the need and desire to praise Him.

> *And some of the Pharisees in the crowd said to him, "Teacher, rebuke your disciples." He answered, "I tell you, if these were silent, the very stones would cry out" (Luke 19:39-40).*

God desires our love, gratefulness, acknowledgment, and invitation. He wants us to crave His presence so much that we can't hold back our praise. He wants us to sacrifice ourselves, our time, and our thoughts to Him, and He wants us to stop thinking about ourselves and make Him the center of our lives.

> *The LORD is my strength and my song, and he has become my salvation; this is my God, and I will praise him, my father's God, and I will exalt him (Exodus 15:2).*

Being Grateful

> *For "In him we live and move and have our being"; as even some of your own poets have said, "For we are indeed his offspring" (Acts 17:28).*

Living a life of gratitude to the Lord is not easy. True thankfulness and gratitude are often lost in our busy lives. Sometimes it seems that non-Christian younger generations don't consider gratitude a worthwhile or necessary emotion at all. To them, good things are deserved and therefore gratitude is unnecessary.

Worldly gratitude seems to be a passing emotion that pops up quickly when something good happens and disappears just as quickly. We are taught at a young age to say thank you. When someone opens a door for us, we say thank you. When we are given a gift, we say thank you. But saying thank you to the one in whom we live and move and have our being should not be as shallow.

Giving thanks is also part of acknowledging God's power and majesty. He has asked us to pray "thine is the kingdom and the power and the glory forever." Thank God that this is a true statement, or we would be forever lost.

Give thanks in all circumstances; for this is the will of God in Christ Jesus for you (1 Thessalonians 5:18).

Living a grateful life is easy when things are going well. When our jobs are going smoothly, the family is all getting along, and we have enough money to pay bills and take a vacation, we can be the most verbally thankful Christians around. Or we may forget to thank God altogether for these blessings.

However, in negative situations, when we lose our jobs, or worse, when money is tight and family fighting rules the day, where is our thanks then? Being asked to be grateful on those days seems unreasonable. No one would be grateful when terrible things are happening, would they? But this is what God desires and deserves.

And let the peace of Christ rule in your hearts, to which indeed you were called in one body. <u>And be thankful</u> (Colossians 3:15).

When we have peace from Christ in our hearts, it is because

we have faith that He is working in our situation. With faith and peace, we can be grateful in all situations but only with the help of the Holy Spirit. When life is hard, we must ask for more faith and peace so that we can be truly thankful for our circumstances, no matter what they are. Faith only grows in difficult times.

We have so much to be grateful for. We have been redeemed. We have been made new, and we will spend eternity with our Father who is in heaven. We are free from sin and death. Yes, life here is difficult and sometimes unbearable. We cry and moan in pain and we are afraid, but we can live a truly grateful life in Christ knowing that nothing here can steal our salvation and that God will meet our needs. He has all power!

So we can confidently say, "The Lord is my helper; I will not fear; what can man do to me?" (Hebrews 13:6)

God is working in our lives all the time. We are exactly where He wants us. We are learning exactly what we need to learn. We are perfectly in His time and in His hands.

The Lord is my strength and my shield; in him my heart trusts, and I am helped; my heart exults, and with my song I give thanks to him (Psalm 28:7).

Let us not be stingy with gratitude to the Lord. Either we believe that He is good all the time or we don't. If we believe that God is good and that He is working all things for the good of those who love Him, then we must express our gratitude, even when we do not feel it.

Setting our eyes and hearts on things that truly matter, we will be assured that we have been given everything that is important in the universe. Let us show God and the world just how grateful we are for His great love, power, glory, and Kingdom.

Oh give thanks to the Lord, for he is good, for his steadfast love endures forever! (Psalm 107:1).

Take Up Your Cross

And he said to all, "If anyone would come after me, let him deny himself and take up his cross daily and follow me" (Luke 9:23).

To truly follow Christ, we must take up our cross. Jesus died on the cross for our sins and rose from the dead so that we could be forgiven and spend eternity with Him. But many may find it interesting to notice that Jesus mentioned to the disciples that they would need to take up the cross and follow Him before He was crucified on the cross. He also told this to the rich young ruler.

He hadn't been crucified yet, and His disciples never asked Him why He used that phrase. They already understood it.

Then Jesus told his disciples, "If anyone would come after me, let him deny himself and take up his cross and follow me" (Matthew 16:24).

They didn't understand that He would be nailed to a cross. Not until the end of Christ's ministry did they realize that He was to be crucified. But the phrase 'take up your cross and follow me' held particular meaning to the people of that day.

Today we hear people talk about 'their cross to bear' when describing some burden or hardship in their lives. But this is not what was meant in Christ's day when He spoke to His disciples. The cross at that time was known as the most horrible of punishments. It was used to put people to a slow and agonizing death for their actions or their beliefs. The criminals were required to carry their own crosses uphill to their death.

Whoever does not bear his own cross and come after me cannot be my disciple (Luke 14:27).

It was a well-known means of torture and death. But for those who were not criminals, it came to mean being willing to die for what you believed. It meant and still means today to be willing to do whatever it takes to follow Jesus, even if it means death.

Taking up the cross of Christ is total self-sacrifice, submission to Christ, and the abandonment of our own selfish desires. To give one's life completely over to God through His son Jesus Christ, seeking to be like Him, following His example, and living to please Him is what it means to take up the cross.

And calling the crowd to him with his disciples, he said to them, "If anyone would come after me, let him deny himself and take up his cross and follow me (Mark 8:34).

Little did the disciples know that when Christ said to follow Him by taking up the cross, it would literally mean death and, to some of them, death on the cross. But they gave up their lives, their known existence, and their jobs for Him. They gave up families and hometowns for Him. They followed Him into dangerous situations because they knew His power was from God. They took up the cross for Christ, not knowing that in the near future, Christ would hang on one.

Today we ask God into our hearts, but we assume that it will not lead to death. We don't completely deny our own wants. We don't completely submit to Him. Most of us attend church if it is convenient but separate our jobs and hobbies from our Christian lives. Praise God for His mercy to us, because we are not able to completely deny ourselves for His glory.

> *And whoever does not take his cross and follow me is not worthy of me (Matthew 10:38).*

We need our hearts to be crucified daily making that commitment to take up our cross and be willing to give our all to follow Christ. Yes, we have been saved, but that is not the end. We cannot afford to relegate our Christianity to a back seat in life. The only way to truly follow Him is to be willing to place everything we have, everything we are and everything we love under His control. We must take up our cross and follow the Lord. Even unto death.

> *I have been crucified with Christ. It is no longer I who live, but Christ who lives in me. And the life I now live in the flesh I live by faith in the Son of God, who loved me and gave himself for me (Galatians 2:20).*

Time to Grow Up

> *But grow in the grace and knowledge of our Lord and Savior Jesus Christ. To him be the glory both now and to the day of eternity. Amen (2 Peter 3:18).*

God tells us again and again in His word to grow in grace and in knowledge, and yet many of us remain where we started at salvation. This first step of accepting Christ is only the beginning of a great lifelong journey of growth if we pursue it. At salvation, we are born again. The Holy Spirit has drawn us to Christ, and we have chosen rightly. But we are babies, and He wants us to grow up.

At salvation, we are changed from the inside out by Christ's Spirit. We are now counted among the Christians. We are saved, but we have little experience living a Christian life and we can easily be led astray. Some Christians remain at this level forever, never growing, being tossed about, saved but struggling. God's power through the Holy Spirit and reading His word is how we grow in our relationship with Him.

> *So that we <u>may no longer be children</u>, tossed to and fro by the waves and carried about by every wind of doctrine, by human cunning, by craftiness in deceitful schemes. Rather, speaking the truth in love, <u>we are to grow up</u> in every way into him who is the head, into Christ, from whom the whole body, joined and held together by every joint with which it is equipped, when each part is working properly, makes the body grow so that it builds itself up in love (Ephesians 4:14-16).*

It would be so nice if immediately after we accept the Lord we were taken up into heaven. But no, we are still in the world, and life is pretty much where we left it. We are changed but the world is not. The old world and the old problems remain. We are innocent babes among cunning wolves.

However, as Christians, we have help in this evil world. God's power and glory through the Holy Spirit are with us. We can ask for His will, His guidance, and His gifts. We can mature as Christians by allowing the Holy Spirit to work in our lives.

> *Therefore let us leave the elementary doctrine of Christ and go on to maturity, not laying again a foundation of repentance from dead works and of faith toward God (Hebrews 6:1).*

Christianity is not a once and done thing, and it is not something you keep coming back to repeatedly either ("not laying again a foundation of repentance..." it says in Hebrews). We have already been forgiven; we have accepted Christ. Now it is time to grow in grace and knowledge and go on to maturity. This is not the time to say, "I'm saved and that's all I need."

As this world spirals down into hell, we need God's glory and power to help us stand strong by becoming mature followers of Christ. If we remain babies, we continue in immature thinking and will always be frustrated, wondering why life isn't what we expected.

There is no stopping place, no resting on our laurels thinking we have made it and are home free. Our acceptance of Christ is the elementary doctrine that we are to leave behind.

> *For though by this time you ought to be teachers, you need someone to teach you again the basic principles of the oracles of God. You need milk, not solid food, for everyone who lives on milk is unskilled in the word of righteousness, since he is a child. <u>But solid food is for the mature</u>, for those who have their powers of discernment trained by constant practice to distinguish good from evil (Hebrews 5:12-14).*

It is important to inform new believers that the powers of darkness in this world are not pleased that they have chosen to follow Christ. Satan will do whatever he can to keep us weak and uneducated, liable to fall away at any minute.

He keeps us focused on our own problems so that we cannot reach others for Christ. He will make us fearful, ignorant, and unable to accomplish anything for God.

> *"... until we all attain to the unity of the faith and of the knowledge of the Son of God, to <u>mature manhood</u>, to the measure of the stature of the fullness of Christ"* **(Ephesians 4:12-13).**

As our faith and knowledge grow, we not only become stronger in our own walk with God but can bring others into the Kingdom and help them to grow into mature adults. If we have stopped maturing in our walk with God, now is the time to start again. Salvation is only the beginning.

Great things await those who seek more and more of God. Talk to Him constantly and remember that His is the Kingdom, the power, and the glory forever. We belong to Him.

The world is evil. It is time to grow up and remember that our Father is powerful.

> *"I am the true vine, and my Father is the vine dresser. Every branch in me that does not bear fruit he takes away, and every branch that does bear fruit he prunes, that it may bear more fruit. Already you are clean because of the word that I have spoken to you. Abide in me, and I in you. As the branch cannot bear fruit by itself, unless it abides in the vine, neither can you, unless you abide in me. I am the vine; you are the branches. Whoever abides in me and I in him, he it is that bears much fruit, for apart from me you can do nothing" (John 15:1-5).*

Chapter Eleven

Amen (So Be It)

Belonging

My friends scorn me; my eye pours out tears to God (Job 16:20).

There are times in church groups that we may feel alone. When others are laughing and talking and we are not included, our insecurities come out in full force. It happens to us all. Others may not show it, but it happens.

We don't show our feelings of aloneness, but inside, we may wonder what is wrong with us since everyone else seems so happy. Human beings need to belong. Even the shyest of people are not meant to be alone in church. Most people long to fit in and yet often feel like outsiders among Christian brothers and sisters, especially those who are introverts.

What is this feeling that overcomes us and why do we experience it? Where could we belong more than at church with others who believe in our Almighty God?

For in one Spirit we were all baptized into one body — Jews or Greeks, slaves or free — and all were made to drink of one Spirit (1 Corinthians 12:13).

This feeling of not belonging can attack any one of us at any time. It is a profound feeling of loneliness while surrounded by others. These emotions make us question our worthiness and wonder if others see us as unattractive, not friendly, or arrogant. The church is supposed to be a family but often doesn't feel like one. Is this the Amen of church? No.

We are all different. We are of different age groups, different jobs, or no jobs. Some have children. Others travel. We have different interests and spend our weeks in various activities. Some go to Sunday School and Bible studies. Some attend every church activity while others can't or don't want to. We are all at different levels of maturity in our relationship with God. We have different talents and different ideas about how things should be. We are different parts of the Body of Christ.

And he gave the apostles, the prophets, the evangelists, the shepherds and teachers, to equip the saints for the work of ministry, for building up the body of Christ (Ephesians 4:11-12).

God created us as unique individuals, giving each of us strengths and specific callings so that His work can be done more successfully. However, human nature makes us more comfortable with people who have the same interests and talents. Therefore, it is difficult to reach out to those who are different.

The Pastor appearing to show preference to certain groups of people can be off-putting and increase our feelings of not belonging to any group. It is the same feelings we had when we were younger and not allowed in a certain 'clique.'

In addition, those who are shy or uncomfortable in large groups may not be sought out because they always say 'no' anyway. Some judge those around them as 'having it all together' and unapproachable, thinking they don't need a friend.

> *"He who withholds kindness from a friend forsakes the fear of the Almighty (Job 6:14).*

As church members, it is our responsibility to be aware of those outside our preferred groups and make conversation with them, taking a sincere interest in their lives. We often get wrapped up in our own lives and want to share them with others who are like-minded. We may walk past one member on the way to another to share a story or say hello.

This is something we must be mindful of, not only welcoming new members but making sure all the regulars feel they are part of the body, even when we don't think they need us to reach out. If we reach out to everyone, even those who seem aloof, we will find that many are very thankful to be sought out. And this is the Amen of church.

> *Above all, keep loving one another earnestly, since love covers a multitude of sins. Show hospitality to one another without grumbling. As each has received a gift, use it to serve one another, as good stewards of God's varied grace (1 Peter 4:8-10).*

Those of us who experience the emotion of not belonging need not berate ourselves. If we feel that we do not fit in, there are things we can do. We can pray that the feelings, which are not of God, will pass and instead become the one who reaches out to others who may be standing alone. The Holy Spirit gives us love and kindness to share. Amen.

> *That is, that we may be mutually encouraged by each other's faith, both yours and mine (Romans 1:12).*

As We Are

For you formed my inward parts; you knitted me together in my mother's womb. I praise you, for I am fearfully and wonderfully made. Wonderful are your works; my soul knows it very well. My frame was not hidden from you, when I was being made in secret, intricately woven in the depths of the earth. Your eyes saw my unformed substance; in your book were written, every one of them, the days that were formed for me, when as yet there was none of them (Psalm 139:13-16).

We have all heard the phrase "God loves us just the way we are." Is it true? Is it possible? Doesn't He want us to change and be better? We have so many faults. We are evil and sinful. We listen and follow the evil of this world without even knowing. Before we come to know Christ, we are lost in sin.

The statement of His love is true. Though He may be dismayed at our behavior at times, He still loves the children He created. We do not stop loving our children when they misbehave and neither does our heavenly Father. God's word assures us that He loves His creation more than we could ever understand, and He will never turn away. His love is unconditional. "For God so loved the world..." (John 3:16).

For those who have not turned to Him, He stands by continually knocking at the door of their hearts to be let in. They (or we) do not have to become "good enough" before accepting Christ. He knows our sins! He knows us!

There is no hiding who and what we are from God, but He wants us anyway because He made us. When we come to Him, He cleanses us from all unrighteousness and creates in us a clean heart. His Holy Spirit will teach us and lead us. He loves us while we are yet sinners.

> *Behold, I stand at the door and knock. If anyone hears my voice and opens the door, I will come in to him and eat with him, and he with me (Revelation 3:20).*

Those of us who have already come to Him are not perfect. We will not be until we enter the Kingdom of Heaven. We all have much to be forgiven for daily. We think badly of others, argue, fight, lie, and do things knowingly that are not right. But the Holy Spirit continues to work in our lives as we grow closer in our relationship to God.

We are all created for God's work. He desires that Christ's blood redeems everyone and brings us back into a close relationship with Him. We lost this relationship in the Garden of Eden, and God wants it back.

The only way for us to be redeemed and our relationship restored was for Christ to die on the cross in our place. We deserved to die for our sins, but He died for us as the last and final blood sacrifice. Whether we have come to accept this gift yet is not what makes God love us. God does not love only Christians. Amen.

> *For we are his workmanship, created in Christ Jesus for good works, which God prepared beforehand, that we should walk in them (Ephesians 2:10).*

God loves us, not our lifestyles. He loves those who are homosexual or straight, Democrat or Republican, and any race, creed or religion. That does not mean that we are all going to spend eternity with God by no means, but we all can choose to do so by turning from sin and following Christ.

Choosing to follow Christ does not make God love us more. It makes Him rejoice because choosing to follow Christ redeems us in His sight. His love, however, is constant and never changing.

We are all the works of God's hands. Not one of us is better than another though we, in our human weakness, may think so. Each of us was made by God to be ourselves. Our lives were shaped by our upbringing, experiences, and choices.

We are free to make choices that are not pleasing to God, but He created us with certain personalities and skills that are perfect to work for His glory. Once we choose Him, our true purpose can begin. For now, and always God loves us just the way we are. Amen.

Did not he who made me in the womb make him? And did not one fashion us in the womb? (Job 31:15).

Let There Be a Change of Heart

Therefore, if anyone is in Christ, he is a new creation. The old has passed away; behold, the new has come (2 Corinthians 5:17).

When we ask Christ (God) to forgive our sins and come into our hearts, He changes us. At the moment of decision, we receive Christ's love and His Holy Spirit and experience a lifting of our burdens. We feel a great desire to start living differently.

Some who begin the journey with God turn away to another path when life gets hard. Not all who choose God will continue to walk with Him. Some may return to old ways and habits. Not building a strong relationship with God daily and not increasing in the knowledge of His word allows the struggles of life to bog us down until it may seem easier to just go back to the way we were. When the evil of the world knocks us over, our newfound faith can falter.

And he told them many things in parables, saying: "A sower went out to sow. And as he sowed, some seeds fell along the path, and the birds came and devoured them. Other seeds fell on rocky ground, where they did not have much soil, and immediately they sprang up, since they had no depth of soil, but when the sun rose they were scorched. And since they had no root, they withered away. Some seeds fell among thorns, and the thorns grew up and choked them. Other seeds fell on good soil and produced grain, some a hundredfold, some sixty, some thirty. He who has ears, let him hear" (Matthew 13:3-9).

Each of us must choose for ourselves how we will tend the seed of the word of God. He gave us instruction in His word, and He gave us free will. We must take the steps needed as God leads us. Along the way, we may need a hand from others, and we always need the fellowship of strong believers, but ultimately, we are responsible for communing with God, building up our faith, and making right choices.

"Hear then the parable of the sower: When anyone hears the word of the kingdom and does not understand it, the evil one comes and snatches away what has been sown in his heart. This is what was sown along the path. As for what was sown on rocky ground, this is the one who hears the word and immediately receives it with joy, yet he has no root in himself, but endures for a while, and when tribulation or persecution arises on account of the word, immediately he falls away. As for what was sown among thorns, this is the one who hears the word, but the cares of the world and the deceitfulness of riches choke the word, and it proves unfruitful. As for what was sown on good soil, this is the one who hears the word and understands it. He indeed bears fruit and yields, in one case a hundredfold, another sixty, and in another thirty" (Matthew 13: 18-23).

In the beginning, God created us to be His children living in perfect fellowship with Him. The tempter caused sin to separate us from our Father. Salvation through Christ brings us back into right relationship with Him. Therefore, when the Spirit of God enters our hearts (and changes it back to its intended form and purpose), we are born again.

Christians old and new must constantly fight against human nature. We must keep the old 'us' down as the new 'Christian us' strengthens. Changing our instincts, addictions, and habits is difficult, but God provided His Holy Spirit to guide and direct us.

"If you love me, you will keep my commandments. And I will ask the Father, and he will give you another Helper, to be with you forever, even the Spirit of truth, whom the world cannot receive, because it neither sees him nor knows him. You know him, for he dwells with you and will be in you" (John 14:15-17).

No matter how long it has been since we first called out to God, we must continually firm up our commitment to Him by the study of His word, by prayer, by fellowship with others, and by allowing Him to give us a new heart and guide our lives.

Living a Godly life takes hearing and understanding God's word daily so that we keep the good soil that is needed for our faith to grow. It takes listening to God as He speaks to our hearts. And it requires giving Him everything and placing Him in the center of our lives.

Only God understands our hearts. He created them and He wants to make them new. For ourselves, we must guard against the evil one who tries to turn our hearts back to stone. For those who return to sin, we must pray and seek God's wisdom. God will continue His work in every life every day. We cannot become lazy in our relationship with the Father, convincing ourselves that we are fine while wandering into shallow soil.

> ***The heart is deceitful above all things, and desperately sick; who can understand it? (Jeremiah 17:9).***

In Closing…

May we always live according to the Lord's Prayer and call on His Holy Spirit for strength and guidance.

The world we live in today is increasingly evil as the time for Christ's return draws near. We must be strong in our faith and not waiver. Christians are being persecuted all over the world, and those of us who live in places where persecution is less obvious can still see it coming.

We have been told by God that these things would come to pass and to be ready and strong. There may have been times in our lives when we didn't feel the need to concern ourselves with the evil that others were doing and talking about. But today is the day we must get serious.

The devil knows the end is near, and he is frantically using every trick to draw us away from the truth. Stand strong. Read God's word. Pray constantly. Lift up the brothers and sisters in the Lord and show God's love to the world. Do not give the devil a foothold of any kind.

Bear one another's burdens. Preach the Good News to anyone who will listen. We will all be together with the Lord. What a wonderful day that will be.

God Bless.

www.ingramcontent.com/pod-product-compliance
Lightning Source LLC
Chambersburg PA
CBHW021103080526
44587CB00010B/361